1 ONLINE COMMUNICATIONS TECHNOLOGY

IT'S FOR EVERYONE NOW

January 2020…

Innovations in internet based correspondences were at that point growing the .skylines of voice and video cooperation when the worldwide pandemic COVID-19 began. Surprisingly fast, the world's biggest work-from-home examination of the data age was sent off. Transformation being the way to endurance, unexpectedly everybody from chiefs to moms, science instructors to understudies, and lead representatives to grandparents had to wander into the bold new universe of online communication.

Let's progression back to that second on schedule. It's 2020...unless you've been hiding away far from civilization, the COVID-19 pandemic has changed the manner in which you carry on with work, go to class, partake in bunch affiliations like places of worship and clubs, and even how you remain nearby loved ones. From shopper video conferencing to business coordinated effort and usefulness, need really is the mother of development. Amidst fast change, online correspondence has landed immovably at the focal point of this "new ordinary" for everybody. Remote workers of all kinds and isolated families across the globe now rely on online voice and video to stay connected.

Even however a web association and a PC are all that is required for intensive lesson in video conferencing, it's not generally that basic. Everything except veteran nerds can feel like "computerized travelers" as they manage the minefields of their first internet based get-togethers and gatherings, confronting obstructions like dropped associations and video with distorted sound while figuring out how to inventively emulate "I can't hear you."

I've composed this book to help perusers, talented and fledgling the same, ace web-based innovations so they can zero in hopefully on finding the numerous chances this more prominent dependence on web-based correspondence can offer.

Through my online course, and the parts in this book, perusers get the opportunity to find out with regards to the best devices accessible, sharpen their online relational abilities, and push their general efficiency forward into the 21st century. As we witness the utilization of online video communication

speeds up to mass reception around the world, with it comes unlimited freedoms for those with a sharp eye for arising trends.

What do you get when you join Zoom video conferencing with school field trips? Blast! Another instructive business is conceived. FieldTripZoom is a real organization that has become so famous, they need to utilize live spilling to oblige a portion of their bigger occasions since they grew out of Zoom.

Merge video conferencing and live real time? Could another syndicated program or a web recording with crowds that conceivably rival that of TV or link organizations? My undisputed top choice is otherworldly sharing and online love gatherings, facilitated by little houses of worship that have observed a much bigger local area than they initially figured it out. More practical maybe for most is the acknowledgment of expanded efficiency through extended correspondence and cooperation opportunities.

This book won't just assist you with finding how to organize your online correspondence innovation, it will urge you to branch out and make your online forte. I will show you the methodologies and best practices you really want to bridle the force of all the most recent video specialized devices to free you to foster new plans to apply to your interesting vision.

I know, change can be awkward, yet the future consistently holds a silver lining for innovators. For instance, the boundless reception of video interchanges has the ability to decrease travel which is positive as far as lessening the world's carbon impression. That is really great for battling a worldwide temperature alteration. There are likewise many mutually beneficial business situations, similar to a more expanded and useful labor force. Furthermore most businesses invite the chance to lessen the expense of office space by growing to a bigger far off labor force. This change might end up saving organizations countless dollars every year on office leases, security, and other related costs.

For some, the present "new typical" includes a lot of working from home and it's probably going to remain as such for a long time to come. Even before the pandemic, expanding the number of remote workers was already a trend supported by many top corporate executives. A new Gartner Organization study (Gartner, April 2020) showed that 74% of (CFOs) overviewed expected to move beforehand on location representatives to remote work for all time post COVID-19. Numerous participating

CFOs indicated that remote work might turn out to be a greater amount of the standard than the special case as organizations hope to reduce business land expenses and better shield their labor force from transferable illnesses.

Simultaneously, as managers hope to receive these likely rewards, laborers also are finding a superior balance between fun and serious activities by utilizing the coordinated effort instruments that permit them to telecommute. Distant representatives can immediately kill the time spent driving to and from work. This time-investment funds might mean greater quality time with loved ones, and that could actually make workers more joyful and more useful over the long haul. Also that is an aid for business and family life.

For companies looking to improve their bottom lines, happy people tend to be more productive. A 2015 study at the University of Warwick (Warwick, ac.uk, 2015) found that happy employees are, on average, 12 percent more productive than unhappy employees. For most workers, an improved work-life balance increases happiness and by extension, improves productivity. The shift to remote work may lead to happier people living in a more productive and environmentally friendly society. Businesses in turn can enjoy increased employee productivity. Now that's a win-win.

This book will audit top video conferencing and online correspondence arrangements, remembering the business objective of expanded laborer usefulness. Where we sit today, having encountered a worldwide pandemic, we observe the reception of innovation has progressed what may have required a long time into only months by sheer need. Organizations all over the planet had to reevaluate and reexamine their interchanges coordinated operations to work with every one of their representatives telecommuting for broadened periods, a pattern improbable to invert at any point in the near future. The Genie is out of the crate, yet as I referenced, that shouldn't for even a moment need to be a terrible thing.

The video conferencing advances this book inspects incorporate Google Hangouts/Meet, Facebook Rooms, Skype, Microsoft Teams, and Zoom. The cooperation innovations this book will reference incorporate Google Chat, the G Suite, Teams, Discord, and Slack. While many organizations normalize with only a couple of these arrangements, everybody needs to foster an essential knowledge of every one of the world's top web-based specialized apparatuses on the grounds that no one can tell which ones a business will use to carry on with work. It's vital to stay lithe, versatile, and prepared to embrace new technologies

applications rapidly. Not to stress, these devices are not difficult to learn, and you'll get them quickly.

Looking forward, in the wake of utilizing a portion of these instruments, it's normal to foster a top pick. I empower this. All things considered, it's your online efficiency. For the occasions you're the host of an occasion, you're steering the ship and get to pick the apparatus that offers every one of the highlights you want to achieve your objectives. In any case, for the occasions you want to utilize a device of another person's picking, I'll assist you with getting comfortable with the correspondences stages accessible today.

Once you've dominated the devices of online joint effort, you'll find out with regards to the social side of gatherings. I'll encourage you how to adjust a known super expertise – the force of tuning in. I'll likewise help you how to take off inefficient internet based gatherings or coordinated effort projects. Basically, you'll figure out how to take advantage of your online time utilizing on the web communications.

There's no staying away from it, as you adventure into the universe of online gatherings, you will undoubtedly be welcomed, or constrained to utilize an assortment of new internet based apparatuses. My objective is that when you're done perusing this book, you'll be ready to evaluate and explore all the astounding internet meeting arrangements from the top suppliers... the ones utilized by the most ground breaking organizations. Then it's up to you to decide which of these tools is best for you and your team.

Are you prepared to begin? How about we quit wasting time and dive into the basics online communicators need to know.

2 FIRST A LITTLE BACKGROUND. HOW COULD WE GET HERE?

In merely seconds, a web-based pursuit will observe many correspondence applications you can introduce on your cell phone, PC, or tablet. Each help vows to be awesome, most natural answer for online correspondence with family, companions, and colleagues. It's never been more straightforward or more helpful to communicate something specific, share an image, or interface eye to eye with others all over the planet. But it wasn't always this way.
The specialized devices of today are the consequence of an advancement of mechanical developments that traverses a few decades.

The most punctual web-based talk informing and email applications, as AOL,

MindSpring, and Yahoo, were at first simply accessible to little gatherings of PC proprietors. Have a go at envisioning when sending a text or email between two PCs was very interesting. Quite a long time ago, the best way to send a text (IM) was by message, Telex, or fax. Could it be said that you are mature enough to recall? Reasonable, twenty to thirty year olds and Gen Z have never at any point known about these methods.

Instant messages (IMs) and email addressed the main flood of online interchanges. Texting originates before the web and not at all like numerous different advances, IMs and email stay significant today. These two strategies for correspondence were significant structure squares of the "innovation stacks" (arrangements of administrations worked to run on a solitary application) for online correspondence and coordinated effort. Like an antiquated call, texting and email which basically work something similar, with a couple of added fancy odds and ends, have been modernized however never replaced.

The web (a worldwide arrangement of interconnected PC organizations) has changed the worldwide correspondences scene more than some other innovation. In 1993, two-way communications on the internet represented only one percent of all communications. By 2000, that number expanded to 51 percent and by 2007, that number had move to 97 percent (Hilbert, 2011). At the point when the world's correspondences moved on the web, numerous new business openings arose. From online media to advanced publicizing, economies all over the planet have prospered as sponsors of this enormous movement.

As the web extended, Software as a Service (SaaS), and distributed computing, (off-premise information warehousing) arose. SaaS is the point at which a supplier has an application, making them accessible on-request by membership to clients over the web, rather than downloading them to their nearby or organization drive. SaaS models incorporate the Google G Suite, Slack, Office 365, Dropbox, and Zoom. Suppliers like Amazon, Google, and Microsoft have assisted organizations with conveying SaaS by means of distributed computing innovation, empowering them to offer an assortment of new and strong front-end programming applications. Conveying programming by means of the cloud has made organizations more lithe and scalable.

For the buyer, cloud arrangements kill numerous boundaries to section where individual and undertaking programming are concerned. The movement to the cloud permits suppliers to leave costly, once buys in the set of experiences books while offering clients more reasonable month to month memberships.

This likewise permits buyers to embrace items all the more quickly and in steadily expanding numbers. Because of distributed computing, SaaS suppliers can refresh their items with phenomenal speed, permitting them to stay aware of changing shopper requests. The adaptability of cloud-based arrangements has changed customer assumptions. Suppliers currently should smooth out the organization of new items and administrations to offer consistent gadget cross-similarity to contend. Overseeing programming arrangements in the cloud additionally empower organizations to join their administrations to shape multipurpose stages like, for instance, making a Google Meet mix straightforwardly inside Gmail. Moreover, Application Programming Interfaces (APIs) enable organizations to coordinate outsider programming into these administrations for boundless customization and the improvement of genuinely interesting programming solutions.

Concurrently with SaaS advancements, both IM and email kept on filling in ubiquity as organizations went "paperless." Then, in 2003, Skype video conferencing sent off and immediately became one of the primary video answers for appreciate overall reception. Skype highlighted the capacity to have sound and video correspondences between upwards of 25 guests which was a distinct advantage. Skype's advancement is additionally generally huge because of its development ease of use. By 2004, Skype had logged 1.5 million downloads and 100,000 simultaneous clients (Skype, 2012).

Following seven fruitful long periods of development, Microsoft obtained Skype in

2011. Two years later the buy, Google entered the market with "Home bases." Hangouts was Google's first video specialized apparatus and it was intended to run inside any internet browser on a SaaS model. When Hangouts sent off, Google's Gmail had 500 million clients, and Hangouts, constructed straightforwardly into the Gmail stage, turned out to be in a split second available to a huge client base.

Google before long added new administrations to the stage, incorporating Gmail with other online administrations like Google Calendar, Google Drive, and a set-up of record creation instruments (Docs, Sheets, and Slides). Gmail has accomplished dumbfounding development, and everything started by offering free email administrations. Google has utilized the email administration. Google has involved the help as the entryway for over 1.5 billion clients to get to Hangouts. To place this into viewpoint, in January of 2012, there were 350 million Gmail clients. By October of 2018, only six years after the fact, Gmail announced over 1.5 billion users.

Microsoft's Skype and Google's Hangouts have reliably driven the internet based correspondences industry since the start of the 21st century. Microsoft and Google each deal a comparative set-up of online coordinated effort instruments. In 2006, Google delivered its "G Suite" membership administration, a focal cloud-based work area for joint effort, stockpiling, and interchanges. After five years in 2011, Microsoft delivered its cloud-based usefulness suite, "Office 365." By 2019, Microsoft revealed its Office 365 item had arrived at 180 million clients. In 2020, Google's G Suite client base had outperformed two billion.

Since obtaining Skype in 2003, Microsoft has seen numerous cycles of video conferencing administrations. Microsoft kept on overhauling its online specialized instruments for business purposes with Skype for Business, a retooling of Microsoft Lync. Then, in 2017, Microsoft announced it would phase out Skype for Business and replace it with Microsoft "Teams."

Teams consolidates the best components of Skype's video conferencing arrangements with a more strong group based way to deal with online correspondences that incorporates strung discussions and channel-based venture collaboration.
These progressions basically mark the division of Microsoft's conferencing arrangements into a purchaser rendition of Skype with Teams as the primary video conferencing answer for business.

Google's video correspondence arrangements have additionally gone through significant
changes. Google reported that it would get rid of Google Hangouts for Google Meet beginning in 2020.

As Google and Microsoft kept on extending their cloud-based usefulness contributions, numerous different players in the expert video conferencing space likewise thrived. These incorporate Bluejeans, GoToMeeting, WebEx, and Zoom among others. GoToMeeting and WebEx were early cloud-based video conferencing arrangements that assisted with finishing a time of costly equipment based video conferencing arrangements. Cisco sent off WebEx in 2007 a couple of years later Citrix appeared GoToMeeting in 2004.

In 2011, a previous WebEx engineer named Eric Yuan shaped one more video conferencing organization called Zoom. Zoom sent off in 2013, as the primary video conferencing arrangement configuration highlighting a video-first methodology with an easy to use meeting control bar. Zoom slowly became known as the reasonable option in contrast to its expert internet based interchanges contenders with estimating set at $9.99 each month per client. In 2015 for instance, a GoToMeeting permit cost $39.99 per client each month, while Zoom valuing was under $10 each month for a similar product.

But it wasn't only cost would make Zoom the predominant video conferencing programming supplier by 2020. Zoom's notoriety for usability and unwavering quality developed its portion of the overall industry, as more organizations and individual clients exchanged over from options. In the tech business, an application like Zoom is designated "tacky" in light of the fact that once clients attempt it, they stay with it and offer it with others.

Sticky Zoom was unmistakably situated when the world's biggest work-from-home undertaking detonated welcomed on by a worldwide pandemic. Zoom's "freemium" permit model permits individuals to begin utilizing the item free for coordinated calls while tempting them to move up to paid designs to get to extra elements. At the point when the third or fourth guest enters a gathering without a paid record facilitating the gathering, the gathering is confined by a 40-minute time limit. Zoom's item situating and "freemium" model has surprised the world. At present, a Zoom proficient record begins at $14.99 for gatherings of nine clients or less and $19.99 for bunches with more than 10 users.

Because of Zoom's market predominance, in April 2020 Google chose to make it's Meet video conferencing administration free for Gmail clients with no time
limitations for up to 100 gathering members. In the same month, Google said it's Meet product added three million new users daily, growing by a factor of 30x during the coronavirus pandemic. Not to be forgotten about, during this time Facebook further developed its current Messenger item to help up to 50 video guests with another item send off called Rooms (Fortune, 2020).

By and large, in any case, online interchanges have seen generally sluggish yet consistent development in client reception in the course of recent many years. All the more as of late, the advantages of shared web-based work areas and low month to month client costs have pushed numerous associations to the cloud with record development in reception. While early innovation adopters unquestionably helped spread the worth of online correspondences, nothing could've pushed the business forward more quickly than commanded cover set up orders all over the planet which constrained large number of individuals to telecommute. This prompt and absolute requirement for productive web-based correspondence and powerful coordinated effort is driving advancement to each side of the cutting edge workforce.

3 The Tools Were Just the Beginning: Essential Ideas for Online Communicators

Suffice to say, interchanges have changed significantly in the 21st century. The smartphone has made instantaneous access to information commonplace and small internet-connected devices such as tablets have put instant messaging, voice, video, and data access into the hands of millions in a relatively short period. Correspondences have advanced quickly however with such countless developments happening Simultaneously, there are not many clear rules in how people and groups can best utilize these advances to turn out to be more useful. At the same time, we have encountered a social shift, the universe of work is adjusting to convey adaptable, easy to understand interchanges administrations.

Daniel Pink, the creator of To Sell Is Human, has uncovered enlightening exploration that can assist us with bettering comprehend the changes occurring in the cutting edge work environment. Pink's examination shows that all things considered, 40% of most laborers' time is spent "persuading, convincing, and affecting others." Pink's first-of-its-sort research shows that cutting edge laborers have been approached to foster abilities that cross customary departmental limits to expand efficiency. Pink contends that a "expansive reconsidering of deals as far as we might be concerned" can assist with clarifying the change in outlook in current correspondence. Pink proceeds to take note of that while just one of every nine positions in the United States are in direct deals, the other eight out of nine positions include what he portrays as "non-deals selling" (Pink, 2019).

Modern Workforce Transformation

40% of time spent on the job dedicated to persuading, convincing or influencing others.

Collaboration between numerous specialty units both inside and outside of associations is critical to this advanced labor force change. Pink notes two quickly developing ventures, training, and medication, are profoundly engaged with "moving individuals." These enterprises have renamed whole areas, i.e., "telehealth" and "distance learning" on the side of this developing movement.

Modern interchanges innovation has worked with and speed these changes.

Telehealth is the quickest developing space of the medical services framework, as per the American Medical Association (AMA) (AMA, 2019). In the field of training, a review by the Online Learning Consortium (OLC), distributed before the COVID-19 flare-up reports that distance learning had been developing each year for a considerable length of time (OLC, 2018). Later COVID-19, teachers from varying backgrounds and ages have needed to rehash and reconsider their instructive cycles to adjust to some type of distance getting the hang of utilizing on the web specialized tools.

Both of these businesses depend intensely on viable correspondence. At the point when correspondence between different specialty units is fundamental, online interchanges become the establishment that associates disseminated teams

whether they're situated across the corridor or the globe. These equivalent specialized devices have permitted the instruction and medical care areas to convey their administrations somewhat over the web. This dynamic, thus, has empowered them to track down new arising sections inside their ventures permitting their groups to incorporate auxiliary administrations into their plan of action that didn't exist previously.

For instance, specialists can save patients the problem of coming into the workplace with straightforward subsequent visits that can be directed over a video meeting. These new arising fragments assist with making their associations more productive and broadened. The virtualization of medical care and instructive administrations has expanded the quantity of administrations these associations can offer and in this way the quantity of individuals they can serve. Subsequently, every one of these businesses is currently ready to produce huge number of new positions each year.

What number more ventures will be changed by online correspondences innovation? One more model is the manner by which the COVID-19 pandemic has constrained the trillion-dollar occasion arranging industry to move totally on the web. My book The Virtual Ticket (2020) surveys the change of the occasions business that had to defer or drop face to face occasions because of COVID-19. The whole occasions area keeps on reexamining its job and go-to-advertise procedures – it should adjust considering the pandemic.

As occasion directors endeavor to sell virtual tickets, their occasions can turn out to be significantly more beneficial and broadened on the web. Arising openings incorporate customized wellbeing and health, as educators, mentors, and different suppliers can bet everything on video interchanges. Could an internet based yoga class with a VIP? A composing course with a main creator? Or then again, a cake embellishing class with a cake gourmet expert? Suppliers like MasterClass were at that point in the market with virtual contributions before the pandemic hit. What's changing presently is the manner by which it's not just with regards to set up associations; individuals wherever are uncovering the force of video interchanges. Thus, it's turning into the standard to be looking for that "mystery ingredient" and exceptional worth add that correspondences advances can help them deliver.

Online devices can assist with improving the manner in which we convey when we apply conventional correspondence standards to the cutting edge gathering. Despite the fact that the manner in which people impart today is definitely not the same as the manner in which people conveyed even only 10 years prior, exhibiting a hearty mission,
developing shared regard, and real correspondence stay the keys to progress.

Online correspondence advances permit you to broaden the span of your asAlong these linesciation's interchanges and reinforce your contributions. So, in the midst of seismic and quick innovative changes, it merits recalling that progressing, powerful correspondence and relationship-building stay the key parts of business success.

Taking this thought, above and beyond, Joseph Pine, the creator of The Experience Economy contends that purchasers esteem labor and products more when organizations plan explicit encounters that go with the labor and products they're advancing and selling. In Chapter 11, we'll investigate the most common way of repositioning your extraordinary deals esteem through useful web-based gatherings that upgrade your clients' involvement in your item or administration. There are straightforward advances that you can take meeting participants through to have more significant discussions and provocative exchange on your topic. Along these lines, look to the last option part of the book for direction on this.

Let's get started...in the following segment, you'll find out with regards to the main capabilities accessible on Skype, Google Meet, Microsoft Teams, Zoom, and Facebook Rooms. As you get familiar with the complexities of every video correspondence arrangement, ponder your goals for interchanges. Contemplate the apparatuses and how you can apply them to the extraordinary requirements of your business.

Part 2: The Technical Review

Now that you have a smart thought of how the present video conferencing and coordinated effort instruments were first evolved, we'll check out the absolute most famous arrangements, their abilities, and figure out how to utilize them most adequately. How about we start with one of the most famous arrangements, Skype.

4 SKYPE

Now that you have a smart thought of how the present video conferencing and coordinated effort instruments were first evolved and developed, we will investigate the absolute most well known arrangements, bring a profound jump into their abilities and figure out how to utilize them most adequately. We should begin with one of the most well known arrangements, Skype.

Topic/Feature	Details
Date Launched	2003. Purchased by Microsoft in 2001.
Price	Free. Credits and subscriptions are required for phone calling.
Meeting Participants	Maximum of 100. More available with Microsoft Teams.
Estimated Monthly Users	300 Million.
Screen Share & Recording	Yes. Video recordings saved in the cloud and available for download within 30 days.
Instant Messaging	Yes. Unlimited file transfer sizes

Can we Skype? The name of the help has become universally equivalent as the activity action word for video talks. Skype's capacity to interface individuals all over the planet has left a mark on the world in the video correspondence space. Since its 2003 delivery, Skype's brought huge number of loved ones together in a basic, clear point of interaction. Microsoft, consistently on the

post for inventive arrangements, gained Skype in 2011 and immediately incorporated it into Microsoft Office, later known as Microsoft Office 365.

Four years later the procurement, Microsoft sent off "Skype for Business," which enhanced its current "Lync" business correspondence programming by extending joining capacities. With Skype for Business, clients experienced Outlook and other Office programming straightforwardly with Skype for Business IM, voice, and video highlights by clicking straightforwardly on a contact (beneficiary) to start discussions or timetable gatherings. Basically, Skype for Business made Lync more useful.

Skype for Business designated proficient clients at an expense, while Skype (for individual use) stayed free. By correlation, while Skype allowed conferencing with up to 25 clients, Skype for Business oversaw up to 250. Skype for Business likewise offered committed video conferencing rooms. These "Room Systems" offered video coordinated effort encounters which included voice, video, and content cooperation through one Skype login.

Lync, Skype for Business, and eventually Microsoft Teams

More or less, Lync was Microsoft's unique business video correspondence arrangement. It transformed into Skype for Business like the way Google rebranded Hangouts into its Meet item. In the latest cycle, Microsoft incorporated Skype for Business into Office 365, its cloud-based efficiency arrangement, Skype stays the most well known choice for individual use as Microsoft Teams joins Skype's uncommon video interchanges highlights with Office 365. Teams also includes collaboration features similar to platforms such as "Slack" (released in 2013) and others. We'll look all the more carefully at Teams and arrangements like Slack in a little. We should return again and bring a more profound plunge into Skype.

A Closer Look at Skype

With Skype, clients can interface up to 50 gathering members in High Definition (HD) video quality. Skype video calls incorporate instinctive screen sharing and informing highlights that supplement the gathering experience. The Skype informing highlight permits clients to visit, share pictures, and use "@" notices to get other clients' consideration. Skype's informing stage can be utilized freely from its video conferencing mode. While it's frequently used

as a talk arrangement, clients can change to a video call at whatever point necessary.

Video Recordings

Skype calls can be recorded for audit later. Start a Skype recording by squeezing the button in the base right-hand side of the screen and select Start Recording. Skype accounts are put away in the cloud for 30 days and are accessible for download straightforwardly through the Skype programming. When your gathering is finished, click the More Options button and select Save As to download the recording onto your PC's hard drive.

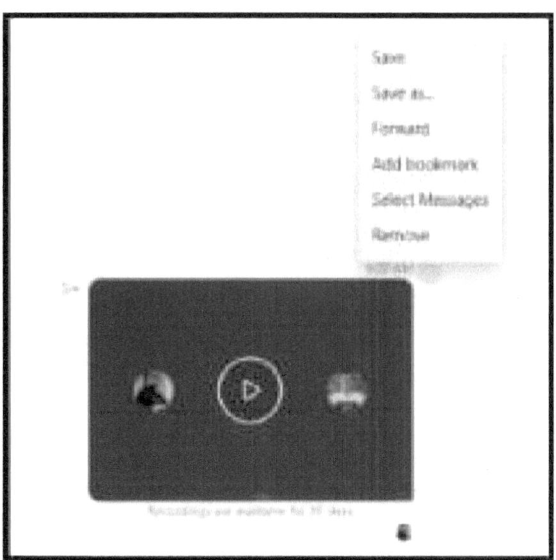

Phone Calling

Skype to Skype sound calls have forever been free. But Skype phone calling also enables you to reach people who aren't online. Calling somebody by means of a telephone number requires Skype credits. Clients can likewise join to get a Skype telephone number in the event that they don't as of now have one. Skype telephone numbers permit clients to pay a level charge for limitless calls. In the U.S., for instance, this assistance costs $6.50 each month. Skype phone calling has many of the features traditional phone service providers offer such as call forwarding and voicemail.

Skype Translator

Skype Translator is an interesting new component that performs live voice interpretations. With Translator, clients all over the planet can speak with one another while Skype interprets the discussions between every language. It works by "tuning in" to sound from one side of the discussion and afterward making an interpretation of it into the local language of the individual on the opposite finish of the video meeting as well as the other way around. Thusly, clients can have discussions with individuals who communicate in unknown dialects without a human interpreter present.

As of mid 2020, Skype was capable of deciphering the accompanying dialects by means of voice: English, Spanish, French, German, Chinese

(Mandarin), Italian, Portuguese (Brazilian), Arabic, and Russian, with more dialects, arranged. Skype likewise upholds more than 60 dialects through text interpretation. Message interpretations make an interpretation of communicated in dialects into message that shows up on the screen for meeting members to peruse on the opposite side in their local languages.

Getting Started with Skype

Over the years, Skype has made its instinctive programming accessible for use on cell phones, tablets, PCs, TVs, and the Xbox One. In this part of the book, figure out how to begin with Skype.

Registering

First, you really want to enroll your Skype account. To enroll, visit Skype.com.

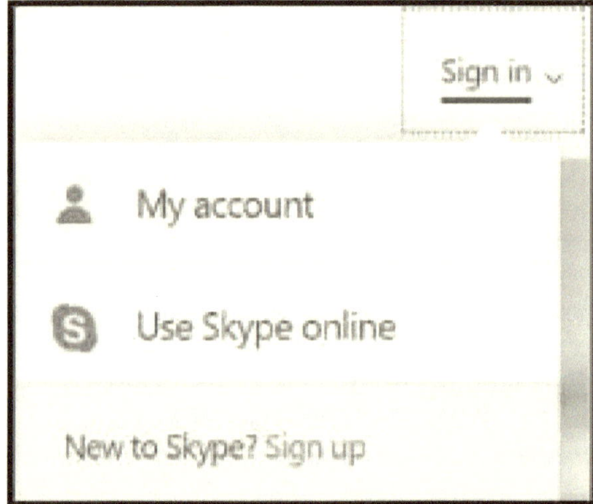

1. In the upper right corner of the site page click the choice to Sign in to see Sign up.
2. Choose the choice to login by means of your Microsoft or Facebook records or use your email address to pursue another Skype account. Marking in with a current Facebook account permits you to interface with companions on Facebook to share, remark, as, and see refreshes from your Friends list.

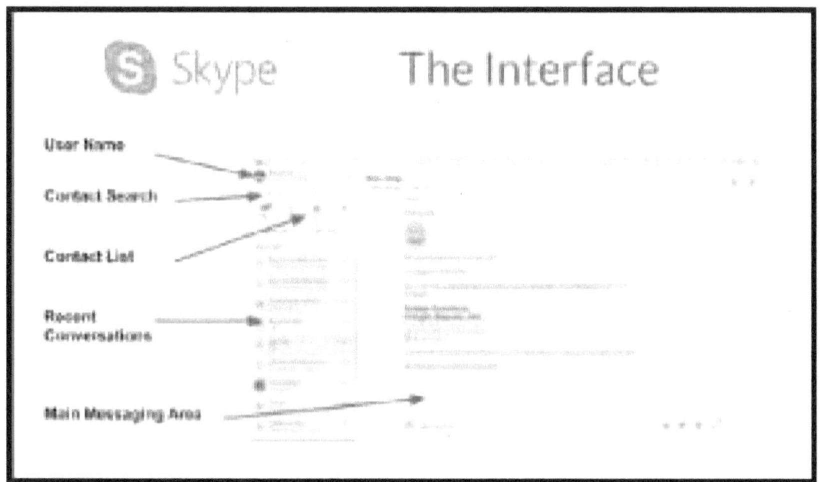

3. Once you're signed in effectively, you can without much of a stretch make a video or voice call with your rundown of companions online.

Creating your "Contacts" or "Companions" list is the initial step to progress on Skype. Therefore coordinating a Facebook account is really smart. You should allow Skype to get to your Friends list, public profile, news channel, announcements, old neighborhood, photographs, site, recordings, and other individual data to utilize Skype with Facebook. Assuming you're not happy with this, don't associate your Facebook account. You can in any case add contacts to Skype without a Facebook account via looking for contacts in the Skype Directory.

Downloading Skype

After making your record, Skype will provoke you to purchase credits. You can avoid this progression on the off chance that you don't have to involve Skype for telephone (voice just) calls.

Mac Users: Download the Mac OS variant of Skype. Select the most recent Mac programming adaptation and when downloaded, double tap the record and drag the symbol into the application envelope. Then, access Skype from the application folder, open the application, create a username and password, and log in.

Windows Users: Download the Windows adaptation of Skype by double tapping a downloaded thumbnail to begin the establishment cycle. When the establishment is finished, open Skype, make a username and secret key and log in.

Android and iOS: The Skype applications for Android and iOS cell phones are comparative. Download the Android form from the Google Play Store or the iOS application from the Apple App Store. In the wake of downloading, send off the application, make a username and secret phrase, and log in.

When signing in interestingly, the application will request that you tweak your language, camera, sound, and profile picture settings.

The Skype Directory

Skype will effectively associate you with a great many individuals all over the planet. On the whole, you'll have to add them as contacts. On the off chance that you endorsed in with Facebook, contacts would show on the left half of the page, as displayed below.

Adding a New Contact

1. Click into the Search confine the upper left corner of the primary page and begin composing the email address, username, first or last name, or telephone number of the individual you're searching for. As you type, assuming the individual has as of now enlisted for Skype or then again in the event that they're in your contacts, their name will show up in the contacts list.
2. Select a contact from the contact rundown to begin a discussion by IM or to make a telephone or video call.

Filter the Skype search bar by tapping the People, Messages, or Group buttons underneath the hunt bar. Messages and Groups are novel to your Skype client ID and will possibly show results assuming you have a Message or Group that matches your inquiry question. At the point when you need to add somebody to your contact show, it's smart to request their Skype ID as this will assist with restricting the list items. You may find multiple users with the same name during a search, but a Skype user ID is always unique. You can likewise recognize contacts by the image related with their record assuming they have one. On the other hand, you can likewise look through utilizing a Microsoft email address.

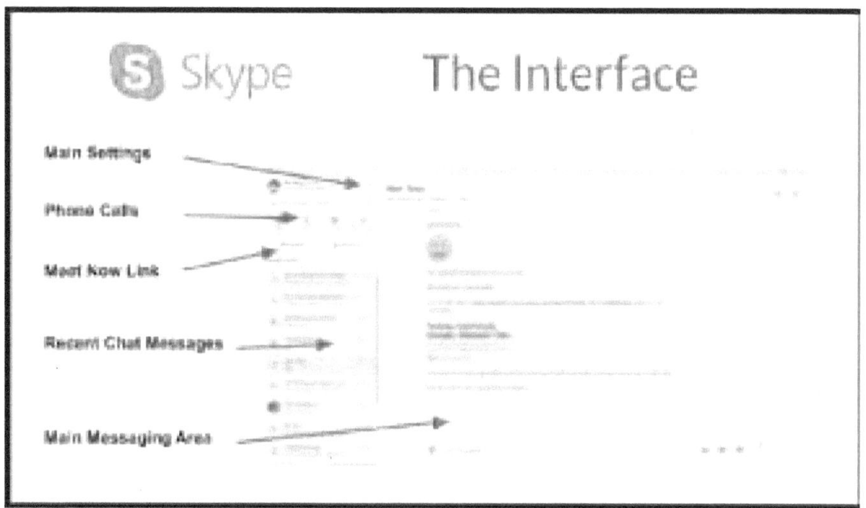

Connecting to Call, Message, and Video Conference

Skype requires the two players required to acknowledge an association. Whenever you first attempt to associate with somebody, Skype sends them a solicitation and when they acknowledge, they're added to your contacts rundown and you're allowed to talk, call, or video conference.

Sending a Message to a Skype Contact

1. Select a Contact from the list.
2. Click into the message box at the lower part of the screen, type your message, and press Enter.

Use this informing region to share recordings, documents, and photographs. Skype has no record sharing size limits which makes it an extraordinary component for cooperation projects.

To call a companion, click the Audio Call/button over the Contact List. This button is additionally found in the upper right corner of the Skype window. To begin a video visit, click the Video Call/button close to the name of the contact.

Meet Now

One of the most straightforward ways of sending off a Skype meeting with anybody on the planet is with "Meet Now" an element that makes an impromptu gathering room you can welcome others into. This element shows on a button over the contact list:

1. Click Meet Now to get started.

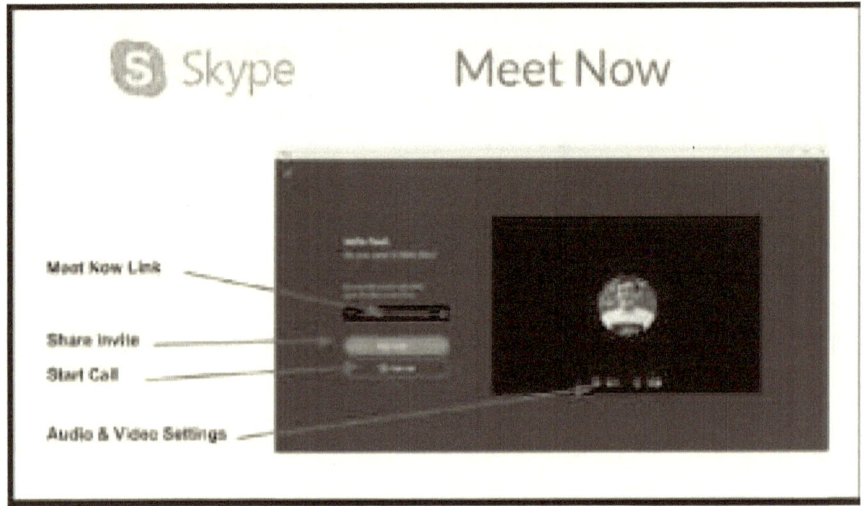

Meet Now quickly dispatches another gathering window with a URL you can email or text.

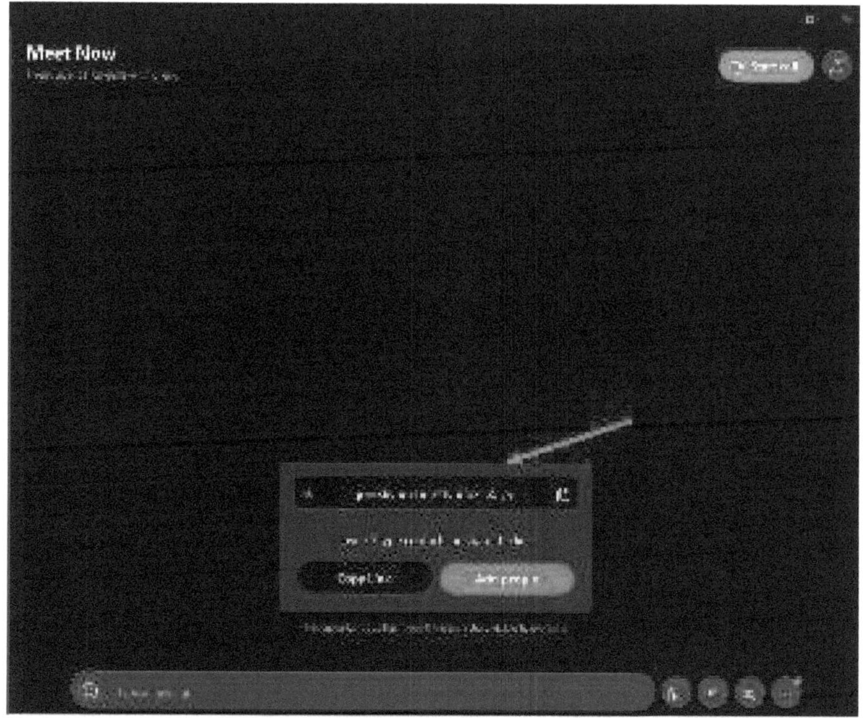

Copy and send this URL to anybody on the planet and they can undoubtedly join your gathering by means of Skype application or utilizing any web browser.

Calls to Landlines or Mobile Phones

The cost of a Skype call relies upon the area of the collector. You'll require Skype credits to settle on decisions; choice to naturally purchase credits when your equilibrium is low. To deal with your credits:

1. Sign into your account.
2. Select your Name in the upper left-hand corner of the screen. Your residual total shows up close to your name.
3. Double-click the dollar amount.

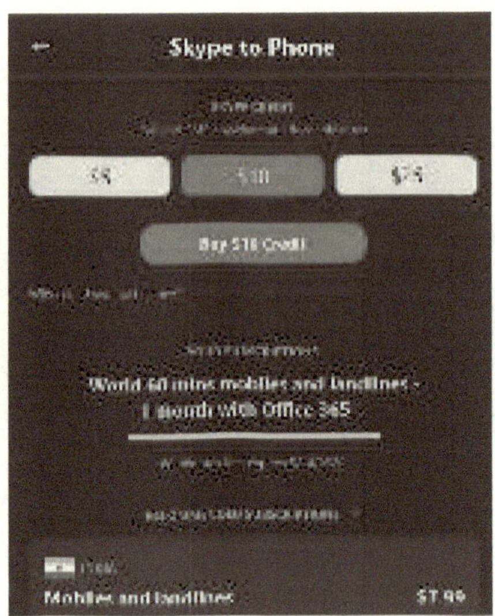

4. Click to purchase how much credit you need and follow the instructions.

Skype Settings

1. To get to Skype settings, click your profile picture and select the Settings gear-tooth. Here is a depiction of each setting:

Account Profile Settings: Account data, including your profile picture, username, and password.

General Settings: Global settings, for example, the application language and availability settings, including interpretation options.

Appearance Settings: Adjust the shading plan and pick among the applications' minimized modes.

Audio and Video Settings: Adjust and screen your webcam and receiver settings here.

Call Settings: Manage Caller ID, Call Forwarding and Voicemail.

Messaging Settings: Adjust things like the message size of approaching messages and more.

Notification Settings: Adjust the quantity of things Skype will inform you about. There's even a "Don't Disturb" setting.

Contact Settings: Manage protection settings and restricted contacts.

Help/Feedback: Confirm which form of Skype you have, survey the current status of Skype, and find connects to extra assets here.

Your First Skype

Before your first video meeting, Skype will provoke you to choose Audio and Video Settings and actually take a look at your mouthpiece and webcam gadgets to decide whether they're working properly.

1. First, check to ensure your speakers are working by tapping the Test Audio button. On the off chance that you hear sound playing, the speakers are working. Assuming you don't hear sound, you might have to choose a new speaker.
2. Next, ensure that your mouthpiece works. Assuming it is, you'll see level pointers move when you talk. Assuming you don't see them, you might have to choose an alternate mic starting from the drop menu.
3. Finally, check to ensure that your camera works. You can see yourself in a little window assuming it works. If not, survey your camera settings.

Tips to Optimize Your Skype Experience

Network Assessment

It's dependably really smart to check the transfer speed of your web connection
prior to facilitating a significant Skype meeting. Transmission capacity is how much information your PC can send and get to and from your web access supplier each second. To decide the transmission capacity of your web association, search "web speed test" on Google which . plays out this test straightforwardly from the list items. Assuming that your video quality is poor, it could be a
data transfer capacity issue.

A data transmission test brings about two numbers – your transfer speed and your download speed. Download speeds are utilized to demand data from the web. Transfer speeds are utilized to send data from your computer.

Bandwidth speeds are by and large estimated in megabits each second. In a perfect world, you need no less than 2-5 megabits each second of transfer and download speed to work a High-Definition (HD) videoconference.

Test with Small Group

Always test your framework before a significant gathering on Skype. Set up a "test" Skype call with a companion or two. Actually take a look at the sign strength of your WiFi association assuming that you're utilizing WiFi with a PC. Whenever the situation allows, it's ideal to hard-wire your PC to an ethernet association.

Right Equipment

The uplifting news about Skype is that it requires next to no innovation. Start with a refreshed PC, admittance to a consistent web association, a USB-associated webcam, and a microphone.

While it's typical to have a webcam and amplifier previously incorporated into your PC, you might need to move up to more excellent webcam and mouthpiece frill. Why? It has a major effect by they way you look and sound.

Host and record a gathering with a companion to explore different avenues regarding what you look like and sound on a Skype call. With Skype, it's not difficult to record a call and audit the video film. Attempt different foundations to show up more expert. What about a shelf rather than a clear white divider? Was your appearance faint or grainy? Turn on more lights or spot extra lighting in the room with the goal that the camera can see you.

Sound quality improves by utilizing a headset mouthpiece. Assuming you're utilizing Skype to record video content for YouTube, updates become critical. When utilizing Skype to record a webcast, for instance, you might need to put resources into a great USB mouthpiece and a couple of headphones.

Webcams include dish, slant, and zoom usefulness. The HuddleCamHD Pro webcam, for instance, empowers you to zoom in and skillet around your space to make dynamic introductions. This webcam incorporates a controller that empowers you to zoom in and outline subjects to show them all the more plainly during video calls. Overhauling your video gear will further develop your video conferencing experience and is a decent investment.

Skype Security

Skype's security strategy necessitates that all clients have an interesting Skype ID which is utilized for validation when joined with a username and secret key, or another confirmation technique. Microsoft deals with its validation servers to check that all gatherings in a Skype call have genuine and remarkable IDs. Skype Messages are likewise scrambled for an extra layer of safety. Some security defects in the Skype framework have been uncovered throughout the long term yet Microsoft has executed patches to determine these issues. Get familiar with Skype Security at https://support.skype.com/en/skype/all/protection security/.

5 GOOGLE MEET

Topic/Feature	Details
Date Launched	It started in 2013 as "Hangouts." Rebranded as "Meet" in 2020.
Price	Freemium. G Suite subscription unlocks all features.
Meeting Participants	Maximum of 250. 100,000 via live streaming option.
Estimated Monthly Users	100 Million. Gmail has over 1.5 billion users; G Suite has two billion users.
Screen Share	Yes. Supports video sharing via Chrome.
Online Workspace	G Suite. Complete cloud-based collaboration workspace.
Unique Feature #1	Cloud/Browser-based platform. No downloads required.
Unique Feature #2	G Suite Integration. Easy to use for G Suite subscribers.
Unique Feature #3	Live Streaming. Easily accommodates up to 100,000 viewers via live streaming.

Today, video correspondence has turned into an indispensable piece of how we work. Without a doubt, for some's purposes, it is the best way to work. Even with so many video communication platforms available today, Google

Hangouts (now Google Meet) is one of the most popular choices, almost by default. Google Meet is a strong aspect of a bigger arrangement of devices. Meet is unimaginably simple to utilize on the grounds that it's coordinated straightforwardly into Gmail and the G Suite. For many people, Google is a gateway to their online experience and its G Suite has become their workspace for online collaboration.

In 2016, Google declared that Gmail had passed one billion dynamic users. Today that number is past 1.5 billion. Every client has free admittance to Google Chat for informing and Google Meet for video conferencing. Notwithstanding Gmail, Google offers video conferencing, informing, and coordinated effort instruments that are amazingly useful for supporting business efficiency from straightforwardly inside the G Suite platform.

The G Suite is a finished internet based work area with famous applications like Google Drive (record stockpiling), Google Docs (archives), Google Slides (introductions), and Google Sheets (bookkeeping pages). Google's G Suite begins at just $6 per client, each month which offers any size business admittance to its arrangement of online coordinated effort devices without restrictive expenses. With such countless individuals effectively utilizing Google benefits, it's no big surprise Google Meet has become one of the most famous video conferencing devices. The following is a gander at administrations G Suite clients can access for low month to month fees.

Feature:	**Basic**	**Business**	**Enterprise**
Price	$6/User/Mo	$12/User/Mo	$25/User/Mo
Gmail	✔	✔	✔
Meet	✔	✔	✔
Chat	✔	✔	✔
Calendar	✔	✔	✔
Drive	30GB cloud storage	Unlimited cloud storage*	Unlimited cloud storage*
Docs	✔	✔	✔
Sheets	✔	✔	✔
Slides	✔	✔	✔
Forms	✔	✔	✔
Sites	✔	✔	✔
Keep	✔	✔	✔
Current	✔	✔	✔

App Scripts	✔	✔	✔
Cloud Search	✖	✔	✔
Data Loss			

Prevention	✖	✖	✔
*Unlimited for groups with over 5 users.			
**Pricing subject to change. Accurate as of May 2020.			

What is Google Meet?

Google Meet is maybe the most available video conferencing instrument available in light of the fact that it's a device that is settled into an assistance that many individuals as of now use – Gmail.

The way that Google's online specialized devices are profoundly incorporated makes for a strong client experience. Google's Gmail is fundamentally utilized for email and, as Skype, clients can make a waitlist of contacts they would instant be able to message, video meeting with, or talk. Steady clients of Gmail have extended their email correspondences to incorporate voice, video, and screen imparting to Google Meet.

Google's "Talk" administration offers strung discussions that clients sort out into channels, like contributions by Teams, Slack, and Discord. Google's G Suite clients observe they team up successfully within a common web-based work area with just a short expectation to absorb information. Online work areas have become de rigueur for associating and working together with remote groups wherever through a basic, available, and consistent interface.

Google G Suite: Google's G Suite is a web-based work area fabricated particularly for online interchanges. Every G Suite client gets a solitary email address to sign in to all of the G Suite instruments. G Suite archive creation devices like Docs, Sheets, and Slides are effectively shared and coordinated among remote groups all over the planet. G Suite likewise handles document stockpiling on Google Drive, cooperation projects by means of Google Chat, and video conferencing with Google Meet. The G Suite likewise incorporates a point by point organization console for IT supervisors who tweak the framework to their association's particular needs.

Google Hangouts: An electronic video talk and informing administration that Google had coordinated into Gmail and is done supporting. Google reported that it will hold Hangouts in 2020 and supplant it with Meet.

Google Chat: Google Chat is incorporated into Gmail. It gives texting a client's contacts. Another Chat highlight permits you to sort out coordinated effort projects into channels called rooms where clients can visit in strung discussions.

Google Meet: Google Meet is the authority swap for Google Hangouts; you can incorporate the free video conferencing instrument into the G Suite. Google Meet backings up to 100 video guests with the free form and up to 250 members with a G Suite permit. We'll investigate Google Meet's significant web based gathering highlights in this chapter.

Google Duo: Duo is a one-on-one video calling application for cell phones and PCs. Intended for customer clients, it's like Apple's FaceTime.

Google Voice: Google Voice is a Voice over IP (VoIP) telephone utility for both home and business calls. It gives a telephone number to send and get calls from any gadget with a web association. Google Voice is sold as an extra to the G Suite.

Next, we'll investigate the particular highlights and advantages of each service.

Google Chat

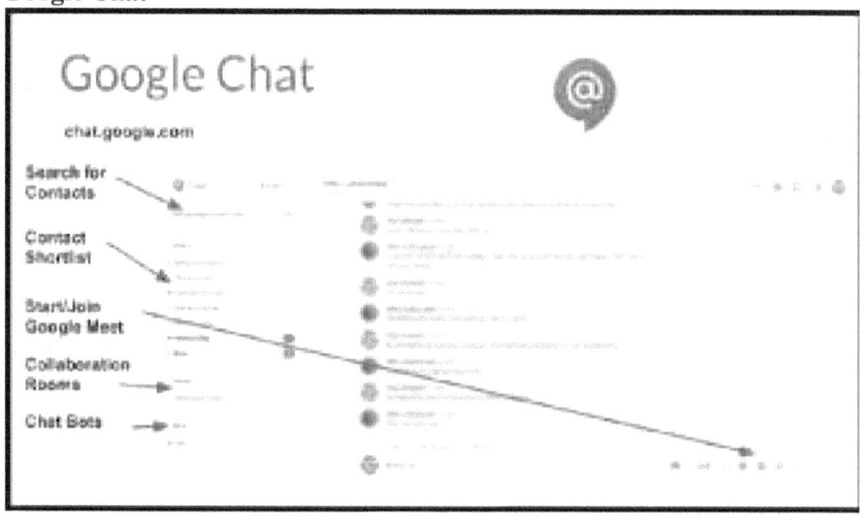

Google Chat is incorporated with each G Suite account and is Google's super texting administration. Free Gmail clients can visit with the contacts they've added to the help utilizing Chat. Furthermore, Chat gives a redesigned insight to G Suite clients with the entirety of the texting and gathering conversation highlights incorporated into Gmail, in addition to the additional component, “Rooms.” The devoted talk work is settled in the Gmail interface, however it can likewise be found at chat.google.com where you can visit with contacts and transform your talks into a voice or video call with Meet.

Chat upholds between hierarchical correspondence between work groups. Colleagues make gatherings of individuals, welcome individuals to take part, and send messages to each other Creating bunches is a simple method for working with group cooperation. Visit coordinates straightforwardly with Google Drive permitting groups to effortlessly share pictures and records inside the point of interaction. Strong drive reconciliations permit clients to tap the Drive button to look through shared documents and offer them.

Google Chat likewise empowers clients to make virtual spaces for each group project that offers the strung discussion groups use to team up. As more groups meet on the web, video telephone calls can assist them with expanding usefulness and adjust on shared objectives to push projects forward. Visit’s vigorous integration

with the whole G Suite permits clients to safely share the records, documents, and thoughts that they’re chipping away at. Associations can without much of a stretch oversee activities and search through group conversations utilizing Google Chat.

Chat clients can likewise look through visit accounts and reference old discussions. You can flip talk history on and off or erase discussions later a particular period for security. You can likewise impede reaches you presently don’t have any desire to speak with. Welcome from contacts outside of your association to Chat on the off chance that they have a Google account by basically composing their email address into the pursuit bar and clicking Send. Whenever they’ve acknowledged, you can utilize Chat and remember them for new groups.

Google Meet

Google Meet is the most recent electronic video conferencing application from Google. Meet is equipped for facilitating gatherings for up to 250 members, and bigger gatherings when live streaming is empowered for up to 100,000 watchers. Meet elements screen-sharing, mediator controls, HD video accounts, and surprisingly live captioning.

Google Meet was intended for utilize straightforwardly within any internet browser. The upper right half of the screen offers an element that empowers clients to open up a

sidebar to see every one of the members in the gathering and visit room. Members with video show up in the focal point of the screen. The settings region, in the base right corner of the screen, permits you to change the gathering design from a default view to a choice of other survey choices. Google Meet oversees and streamlines all parts of the video conferencing experience.

However, Google Meet likewise allows hosts to control the gathering space by offering a restricted arrangement of authoritative choices. Hosts can welcome anybody with an Internet association and an internet browser to a gathering. You can likewise add individuals to a gathering from your contact records in the gathering participant board. One more extraordinary element is the capacity to call telephone numbers straightforwardly through Google Meet.

Sharing the Screen

A focal element of online introductions is screen sharing. Clients can share their whole work area, a particular window, or a tab in Chrome by tapping the Present button on the base right half of the screen.

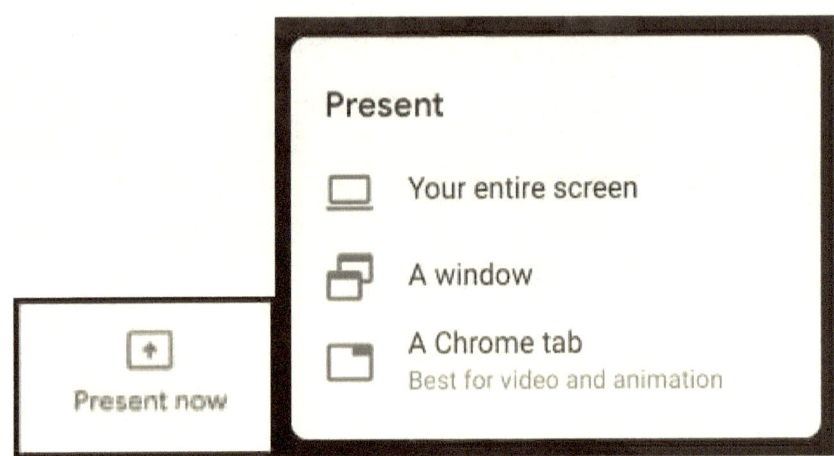

The most ideal choice for sharing a video during a gathering is the "Chrome" tab. To utilize it, just pick a video from YouTube (or any site) and open it in Google Chrome. Google Meet will provide you with a rundown of all tabs open in Chrome to look over. Chrome tabs utilized for screen sharing are shown with a

blue box in the Chrome tab. At the highest point of the Chrome program, you can tap the Stop button to end the screen share.

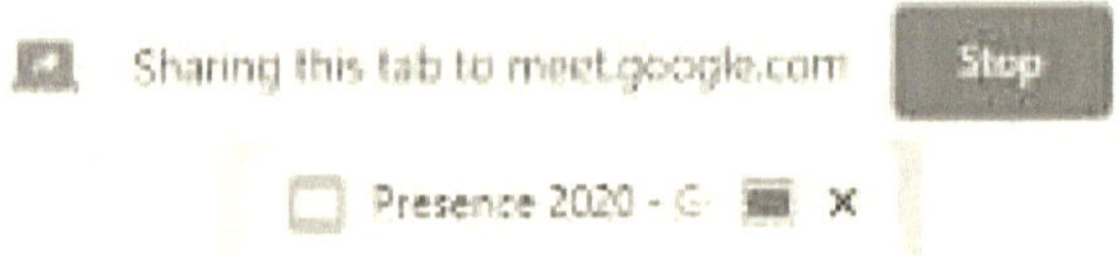

For huge gatherings, Google Meet highlights a tiled perspective on up to 16 members which you can look through in sets of 16. So, if your meeting has 50 participants, scroll through three sets of 16, then view the final two participants on the last screen. For huge city center style gatherings with in excess of 250 members, utilize live streaming, a component you might add by means of Google Calendars.

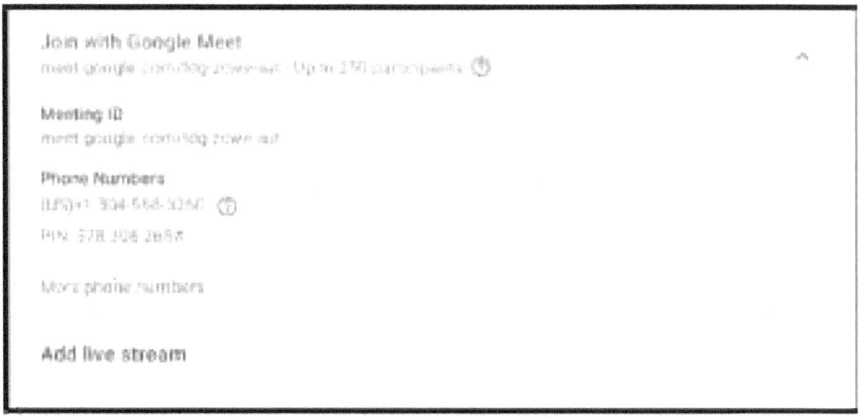

Join with Google Meet

Meeting ID

Phone Numbers

More phone numbers

Add live stream

To add a live stream to a Google Meet meeting, add the live stream as a choice within the Google Calendar welcome. To do this:

1. Schedule a gathering inside Google Calendar.
2. Select Google Meet as the video conferencing choice. This adds the gathering greeting subtleties to your schedule greeting and opens up a choice to "Add live stream."
3. Click Add live stream and your Google Calendar greeting will make a connection to the live transfer that you can impart to anyone

   who needs to watch the meeting.

Advanced Features

Another high level component in Meet is a low-light mode that use progressed AI innovation to detect how your webcam picture can be improved. At the point when empowered, the component consequently chooses when to work on the lighting of your webcam. Google Meet likewise now includes programmed foundation commotion undoing to sift through undesirable clamor. The commotion dropping elements are great for eliminating the sound of composing on a console or a woofing canine in the background.

The Benefits of Google Video Conferencing

Google Meet offers various advantages as an answer for online correspondences. Here is a shortlist:

Accessibility: There are over 1.5 billion dynamic clients with Google accounts, along these lines, probable, your companions, relatives, and associates are now utilizing Google. In addition, Google administrations work on all gadgets and working frameworks, including Android, iOS, Windows, and Mac. Meet is maybe the most open video specialized apparatus on the planet. It gives various highlights and is handily utilized inside any internet browser – there's no compelling reason to download any extra software.

Content: Use Google Meet's recording capacities to record digital broadcasts, interviews, and online classes. Welcome individuals by sharing connections on informal organizations or your site. Utilizing Google Meet, you can likewise live stream to north of 100,000 people.

Cost: Google Meet is free for gatherings with up to 100 clients and the apparatus incorporated into all G Suite memberships. Google Meet is additionally included with all G Suite subscriptions.

How to Access Google Meet?

The least demanding method for getting to Google Meet is straightforwardly through Gmail. Google Meet additionally includes an administration dashboard that is accessible at "meet.google.com." You might get to Google Meet by means of Google Chat,

Calendar, and numerous other important areas all through the G Suite.

Through Gmail

Gmail is accessible at "gmail.google.com." Access Meet and Chat on the base left half of the Gmail screen. From that point, click on contacts to message or call them with the snap of a button.

Meet.Google.com

Access Meet by composing "meet.google.com" into your internet browser. This page shows generally forthcoming gatherings and permits you to snap and join each gathering. It likewise includes a button to send off new gatherings instantly.

Messaging with Chat

Easily start Meet calls with anybody within a Google Chat. Basically click the camera button on top of the Chat message to send a gathering greeting to the individual you've chosen to enter the meeting.

Making a Video Call

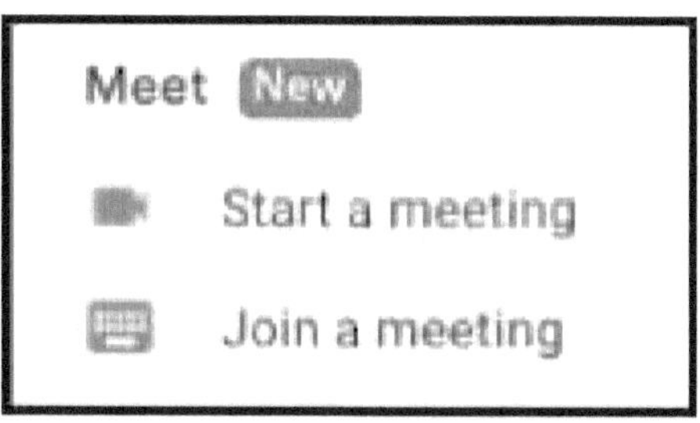

There are multiple ways to start a video call. Most ways to start a Meet call involve clicking a (camera icon) or clicking the **Start a New Meeting** text. Once you start a new meeting, a window opens to invite people to the meeting. When you launch a new video call, a shareable link is created which you can send to other people so they can join the meeting. You can also invite people after a session is started from the meeting attendees' area.

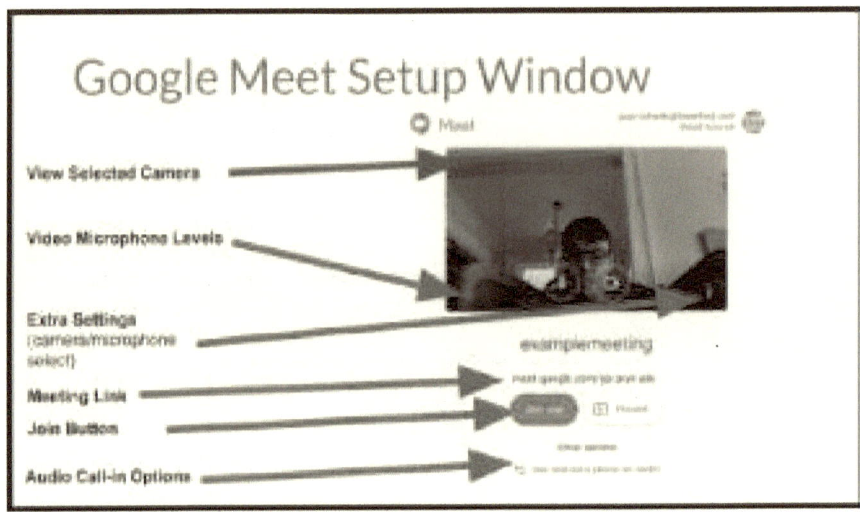

Calendar Integration

Another well known method for making video gatherings is through the Google Calendar application. Make a Google Calendar occasion and afterward add video conferencing to your gathering with the Add conferencing button.

Add conferencing

This element consequently creates a remarkable gathering greeting within a schedule occasion. This empowers you to effortlessly welcome individuals to join your schedule greeting through email.

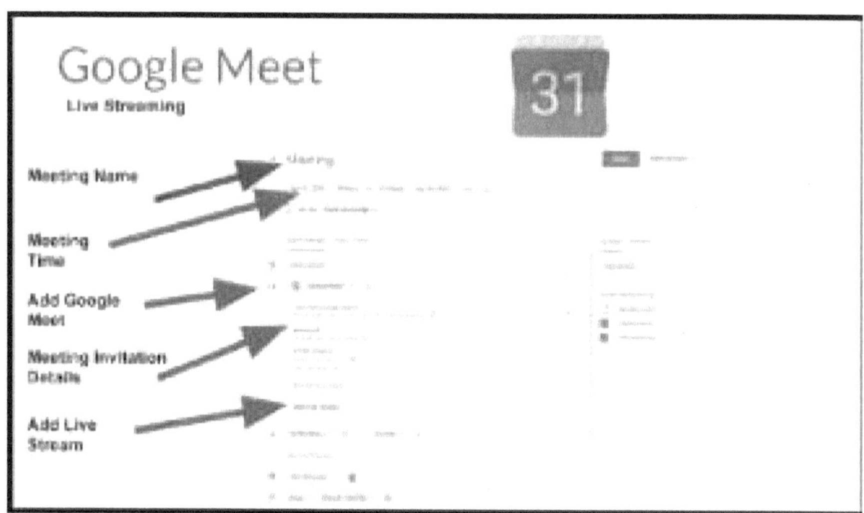

Mobile Apps

Use Google Meet on a mobile phone after downloading the dedicated app.

An icon displays on the bottom right of the screen to start new conversations. Tap it to begin a chat or video call. You can also tap Contacts

to view your chat history. To start a video call, click the icon on the top right of the screen; video call controls are similar to the desktop chat. The Google Meet smartphone app also enables you to share the screen and send documents.

Getting Started with Google Meet

Few bound together correspondence arrangements coordinate a whole set-up of online tools

with telephone, talk, and video calling like Google Meet. Rather than purchasing programming for every one of these capacities, pick G Suite for coordinated instruments like Drive, Docs, Sheets, Slides, and more for a comprehensive experience.

Getting Started

To set up Google Meet on your computer:

1. Create a Gmail account at www.gmail.com. This

makes an email address that is utilized as your Google record to get to other services.

2. Log in to your Google account and type "meet.google.com" in the program. While utilizing the Meet dashboard is great, you may likewise send off video gatherings straightforwardly through Gmail.

3. View your impending gatherings and send off new gatherings from the Meet dashboard.

4. Chat with your contacts at "chat.google.com" or from inside Gmail at "mail.google.com."

Google Meet

Google Meet is G Suite's video conferencing instrument. Throughout the long term, Google blended Google Talk, Google+, Messenger, and Google Voice into a solitary stage called "Visit." You send off Google Meet from Chat to speak with anybody utilizing their email address or telephone number. Whenever you've added somebody to your reaches, you can speak with them separately, or in bunches with these tools.

Video Conferences

The principle capacity of Meet is video conferencing. With Meet there's no requirement for members to download applications or modules. Clients join video gatherings by clicking a connection which saves time. In only a couple of snaps, you can email solicitations, use schedule mixes from Google Calendar, or utilize the inherent texting elements to join a video conference.

G Suite Integration

Few clients are completely mindful of all that Google G Suite offers. G Suite's most famous instruments are its office efficiency arrangements: Google Docs, Slides, and Sheets. It's normal for clients to be comfortable with one, yet not all. G Suite's coordination permits you to plan gatherings with Google Calendars, access visit within Google Gmail, and send off gatherings from Google Chat. From a head's (administrator) viewpoint, client the board for the whole internet based stage happens from the Admin Console for G Suite.

Free G Suite preparing is accessible at

https://gsuite.google.com/preparing/. The Admin Console

G Suite gives a control center to supervisors and administrators to redo the client experience. G Suite Admins access the Admin Console with these steps:

1. Access to the Admin Console is at "admin.google.com." (This is for those with "administrator" accreditations). Contact your IT division on the off chance that you don't have the foggiest idea who your assigned administrator is. Admins can access individual app controls by clicking "Google Apps" and selecting an app such as "Meet" from the list (controls which only display for Admins).
2. Each Google application highlights progressed settings that Admins can change so whole applications can be empowered or incapacitated. A radio button shows close to Meet for administrators to "Empower Meet."
3. Once Meet is empowered administrators should acknowledge the agreements and snap "Continue."

Admin Communication Controls

As a head, you can oversee and control the G Suite. For instance, you may:

- Control whether representatives can utilize Chat with individuals outside of your organization:
- Create an alarm for when clients attempt to contact an individual outside your domain.
- Allow workers to naturally acknowledge solicitations from clients inside the domain.
- Adjust visit history stockpiling lengths or choose not to save histories.
- Enable or handicap video as well as voice calling.

Admin Security Controls

Security settings for the G Suite and Google Meet are "On" by default.

Google pushes security updates to Meet consequently Only the people who start gatherings and schedule proprietors can quiet or eliminate meeting members and support solicitations to join gatherings called by outer participants.

Learn more with regards to Google Meet's security here:

https://cloud.google.com/blog/items/g-suite/how-google-meet-keeps-video-meetings secure.

Most clients won't ever see the Admin Console yet assessing the accessible control choices is a decent way for your association to comprehend the usefulness of this cloud-based work area. Remember the necessities of your association and change the settings accordingly.

Ensure clients take advantage of their G Suite online involvement in strong, forthright preparing. Fortunately, Google Docs, Slides, and Sheets look and feel like conventional applications. Seeing how these devices identify with each other is basic to the total reception of the stage. In cloud-based work areas like G Suite, most usefulness acquires will probably come from smoothing out work processes and expanding correspondence capabilities.

For additional on preparing G Suite clients, in addition to preparing guides and accreditation openings, visit "gsuite.google.com/preparing" for accommodating t.

As an exhaustive, completely included, and practical arrangement, the Google Cloud Platform offers many advantages. But it's not the only game in town and it wasn't first to the plate either. That differentiation has a place with Microsoft. Then, we'll investigate Microsoft Teams.

6 MICROSOFT TEAMS

Topic/Feature	Details
Date Launched	Skype for Business replaced Lync in 2015. Microsoft launched in 2017.
Price	Office 365 subscriptions range from $5 to $20 monthly including Teams.
Meeting Participants	Maximum of 250 with the ability to live stream to larger view-only audiences via Microsoft Stream.
Estimated Monthly Users	200 million monthly users and 500k businesses on the platform.
Screen Share	Yes.
Virtual Backgrounds	Yes.

Unique Feature #1	Office 365 Integration and Threaded Conversation style interface
Unique Feature #2	Robust developer platform allows new application integrations.

Microsoft's Windows has developed to meet the usefulness and correspondences needs of organizations and customers for a really long time. Microsoft has been the worldwide innovator in working framework (OS) advancement since the 1980s. Microsoft can offer adaptable business arrangements that beginning at the OS found on each PC, aside from PCs that sudden spike in demand for Apple's OS. Universally, the Windows working framework is utilized on almost 75% to 85 percent of PCs. This gives Microsoft an upper hand in cloud-based interchanges and work area solutions.

Over the previous decade, Microsoft has utilized its traction in the worldwide OS market to send off Microsoft 365, a cloud-based, work environment arrangement. In 2011, Microsoft set its famous Office items in the cloud, including Word, Excel, PowerPoint, Visio, and Outlook. Very much like Google's G Suite, Office 365's completely cloud-based arrangement is assisting with changing the way individuals work and team up. Groups would now be able to chip away at shared reports progressively as they work together in coordinated interchanges channels. Accordingly, associations have become more useful, better associated, and work processes more streamlined.

Microsoft Teams is the paste that ties the Office 365 instruments together in a cooperative working environment. Groups was intended for online interchanges with incorporations across every one of the main parts of the Office 365 climate. Groups is accessible on most gadgets and effectively associates clients from anyplace on the planet whether they're in the workplace, telecommuting, or mobile.

One of Teams' lead highlights is a strung discussion work, like the coordinated effort suites Slack and Atlassian's HipChat offer. Groups' talk device has turned into a significant and essential resource for organizations with distant workplaces and far off representatives. Groups' capacity to switch between different methods of correspondence make it quite possibly the most famous applications on Office 365.

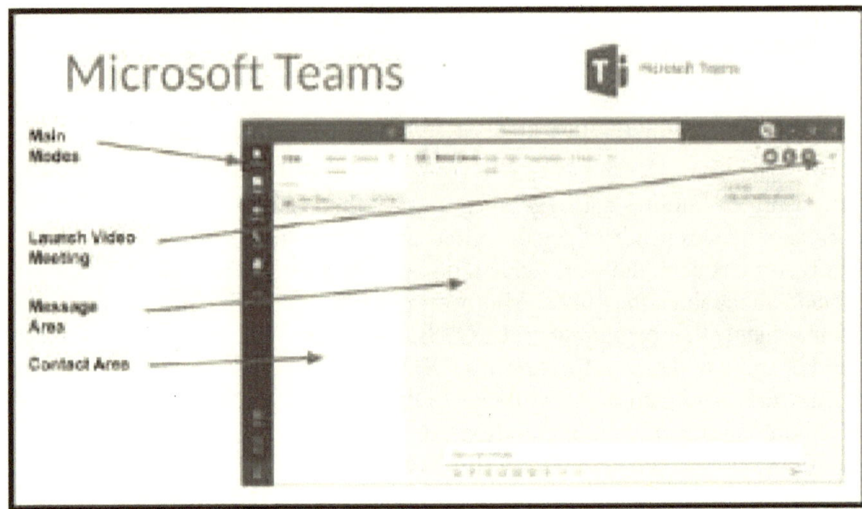

Chat Services

Chat messaging is at the core of Teams. Find **Chat** on the left sidebar button. It allows you to collaborate quickly with individuals or groups of employees by organizing them into a channel to share text, documents, and private files such as images and audio/video calls. Message with people in or outside of your organization securely using the Teams contact list. Organize groups of team members into channels to streamline communications. The interface for Teams is similar to Skype in many ways, making it an easy upgrade path for existing Skype and Skype for Business users.

Notifications

When someone replies to your chat or posts inside of a channel, you're a part of, you receive a notification. User notifications are organized into their tab accessed by clicking the button. Use the activity area to briefly review a news feed of updates for everything going on in Teams. Set up notifications according to your preferences to stay up to date with your team without interrupting your day-to-day workflow. To customize notification settings, click on your profile picture at the top right corner of Teams and select Settings > Notifications. Here's a short list of the notifications that you can adjust:

1. Banner notification show on your PC screen.
2. Email warnings show up in your email.
3. Feed notices show up in your action feed.

Notwithstanding the significant level notice controls, you can likewise switch off notices for explicit channels and conversations.

- Access channel and discussion level notice controls through More choices > Channel notifications.
- To conceal a channel, click More choices > Hide.

Office 365 Integration

Teams are far beyond a basic visit stage – it's coordinated into the most well known Office 365 applications. Clients can share Excel, PowerPoint, OneNote, and Word documents in the cloud, continuously. Putting away archives on Microsoft's OneDrive is a straightforward, viable method for giving concentrated admittance to every one of the documents you want to impart to colleagues in your organization.

File sharing and joint effort are the principle employments of cloud-based work areas like the G Suite and Office 365. Microsoft allows clients to control admittance to their documents on OneDrive. Creators can be certain that all colleagues approach the most recent forms of their work continuously. IT administrators can set their frameworks up to keep a duplicate of significant information on the cloud and a nearby duplicate on a SharePoint server. At whatever point somebody makes changes to a record, the product synchronizes it with the past form and updates it. By incorporating with existing administrations that organizations are put resources into, Microsoft gives security to their activities. Microsoft's cloud-based arrangements are dynamic as in they assist with sending crossover conditions and decisively use both
on-reason and cloud-based working environments.

Deploying Microsoft Teams

Microsoft Teams is conveyed and scaled rapidly in the cloud, not at all like conventional video conferencing arrangements. By moving work areas to the cloud from on-premise arrangements, associations of each size give representatives the apparatuses they need to team up consistently on the web. With membership plans going from $5 to $20 every month per client,

Microsoft's answers remain seriously reasonable. In addition, each Office 365 membership incorporates admittance to Teams. The following is a concise outline of the choices available:

Office 365 Plans	Business Basic	Business Standard	Business Premium
Price	$5/User/Month	$12.50/User/Month	$20/User/Month
Exchange	Cloud	Cloud	Cloud
OneDrive	Cloud	Cloud	Cloud
SharePoint	Cloud	Cloud	Cloud

Teams	Cloud	Cloud	Cloud
Word	Web-only	Web & Desktop	Web & Desktop
Excel	Web-only	Web & Desktop	Web & Desktop
PowerPoint	Web-only	Web & Desktop	Web & Desktop
OneNote	Web-only	Web & Desktop	Web & Desktop
Email & Calendar	Yes	Yes	Yes
File Storage	1TB	1TB	1TB
Advanced Security	Yes	Yes	Yes
Advanced Threat Protection	no	no	Yes
PC & Mobile Management	no	no	Yes
*Pricing subject to change. Accurate as of May 2020.			

Technical Readiness

Obviously, relocation to another stage sets aside time and requires arranging. While the cloud improves on the arrangement of instruments in numerous ways, there are mechanical and human elements to consider. For instance, you'll have to consider network transfer speed and web access which are needed for clients to change smoothly.

Because of these contemplations, it's fundamental to liberally gauge the time your workers should learn and adjust to new programming. Foolish advances can contrarily affect representative usefulness and the proficiency of your business.

Consider remarkable preparing systems for every job in your organization. MicroSoft offers a "Microsoft Office 365 Training Center" which is loaded with assets to help your workers during the on-boarding process and guarantee a smooth progress. Access the Office 365 instructional hub for the

U.S. at https://support.office.com/en-us/office-preparing center

Think of these assets as deskside backing to assist you with arranging preparing for representatives prior to sending Office 365. Preparing will give groups an opportunity to find out with regards to things like new work processes and usefulness hacks. As you change representatives to Office 365, set aside the effort to share your execution vision and clarify the advantages of a cloud-based work area with the goal that everybody comprehends the innovation and is prepared to hit the ground running.

Organize Channels

Carefully plan how interchanges channels for your organization ought to show up inside Teams. Make just however many gatherings as your organization needs to impart adequately. Each gathering should incorporate the perfect individuals. It's lumbering to explore and oversee such a large number of correspondences channels, particularly for new workers. Calibrating bunch diverts is examined more meticulously in Part 3 of this book.

Well-arranged correspondence channels decrease the chance of interruptions for explicit people or groups. To further develop cooperation and usefulness, I suggest looking at the design of your association and how it works together before you set up channels.

Here are ways to make correspondence directs in Teams:

- Understand the inside construction of your company.
- Start little and become the quantity of channels as necessities come up.
- Determine consents, organization, and jobs before you launch.
- Always keep business goals in mind.
- Train representatives on notice the board to permit people to tailor and change their experience.

Who is Using Teams?

Microsoft says, north of 500,000 organizations overall use Office 365 and that Teams is their quickest developing programming arrangement. New Teams highlights incorporate information misfortune anticipation, live subtitles, live occasions, whiteboarding, modified foundations, data hindrances, secure private channels, and insightful catch. Groups is as of now accessible in 44 dialects and Microsoft keeps on adding more dialects to the platform.

Using the Team's Meet Now Feature

Perhaps the easiest way to start a Teams meeting is to use the **Meet Now** buttons integrated throughout the application. You can also find a small video camera/button , nested underneath the Teams conversation area.

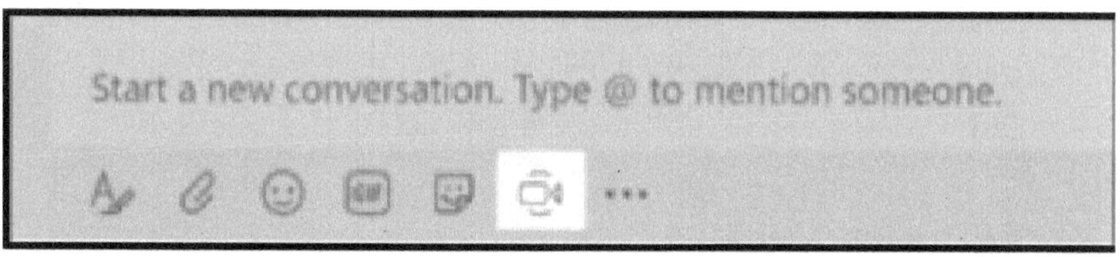

When you click the Meet Now button inside of a specific channel, everyone in that channel is notified. You can also click **Meet Now** inside of a comment. Starting a meeting from inside a comment helps maintain the context of a specific conversation. To do this, click the 

(Reply) button and use the (Meet Now) button inside of your reply.

After clicking Meet Now, a private gathering window opens. Enter a gathering name and afterward choose to either meet in a split second or timetable a gathering for the future.

Once inside a gathering, welcome extra individuals by clicking their names from the idea list on the right-side board. Enter names into the hunt box to find individuals and add them to the gathering. You can likewise add individuals from outside of your association by entering their email or telephone number.

Use the connection button to duplicate a greeting connect to the gathering that you can ship off anybody. Naturally, individuals who join from outside the association are put in a virtual hall. At the point when they show up, their name shows up, and you can concede or deny them access by clicking either the ‘x’ or the checkmark.

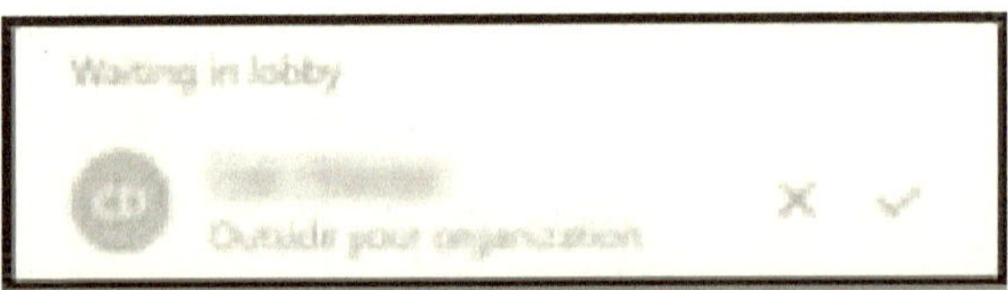

Scheduling and Inviting Participants to a Microsoft Teams Meeting

There are a few ways to schedule a meeting with Microsoft Teams. One of the easiest ways is to use the + New meeting button available in the

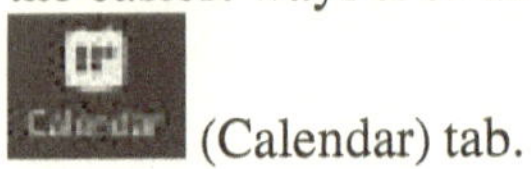

(Calendar) tab.

You can likewise plan Teams gatherings straightforwardly through Outlook, Microsoft’s email framework, or with Exchange, Microsoft’s calendaring framework. Microsoft’s Exchange schedule naturally adjusts with the schedule in Teams. Any place you plan a gathering, it becomes open straightforwardly in Teams or the Outlook schedule. To plan a gathering from the talk window of a Teams channel, select the schedule symbol found in the chatbot. The left-hand side of the application additionally has a schedule symbol that you can use to begin a New Meeting.

After clicking New Meeting, the accompanying window displays.

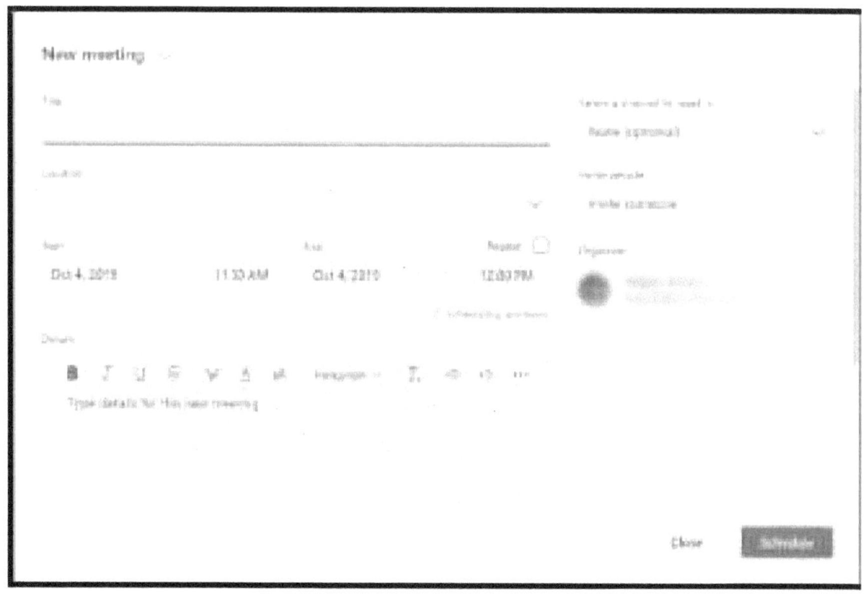

Here, you name your gathering, welcome members, and select a period. Utilize the Scheduling Assistant to figure out an appropriate opportunity when all invitees are free to attend.

Note: To see schedule accessibility with the Scheduling Assistant an invitee should likewise utilize Exchange.

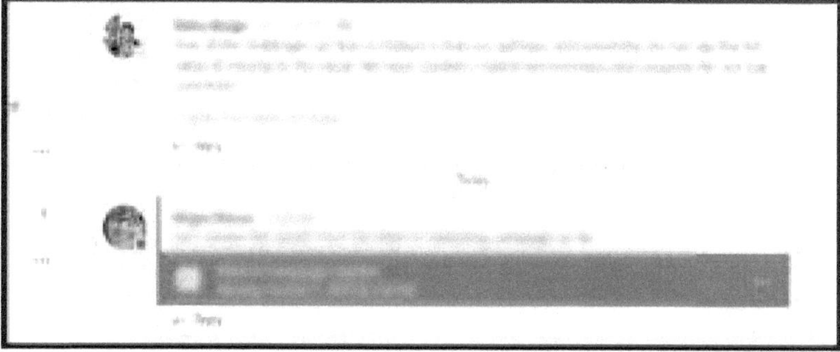

You can likewise choose a channel to naturally welcome everybody in a particular Teams channel to a gathering. At the point when you welcome a whole channel, everybody on

the team will see the meeting in the channels 

and be able to set

meeting agendas, share files, and leave comments on the meeting details. After filling in the meeting details, invite attendees, and click **Save**. Teams will send the notification to every attendee and/or channel with the meeting details.

Schedule Microsoft Teams Meeting from Outlook

You can utilize Outlook to plan a gathering from your Inbox or Calendar. Meeting members can without much of a stretch acknowledge, enter, or view the Team gatherings straightforwardly through Outlook.

To plan a gathering in Outlook, open Outlook and snap New Items > Meeting or utilize the console alternate route Ctrl + Shift + Q. In the subsequent stage, you can add individuals you need to invite.

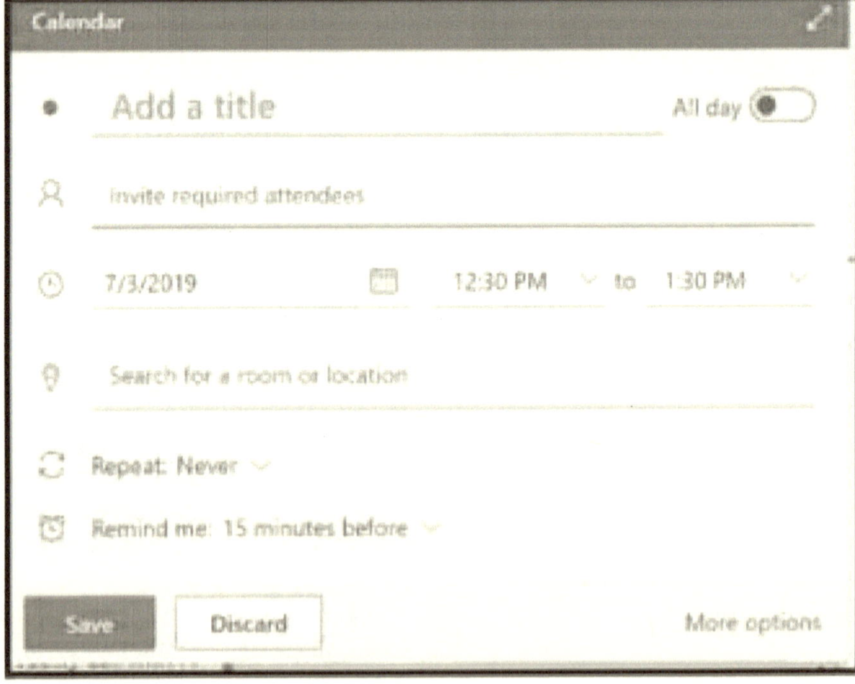

Here you can add a meeting title, invite guests, select a time, and set a location. You can search for rooms or locations to host your meeting. To make the meeting a Teams meeting, click **More Options,** and select the  Teams Meeting toggle. All invitees will receive a notification in their inbox. You can also invite people from outside of your organization. You need to provide the email addresses of any outside guests because they don't display automatically like those from inside your organization. After entering the email addresses, click **Add** to send invitations.

Adding Members to Microsoft Meetings

There are multiple ways of adding individuals to a Teams meeting. For instance, if the unknown "join" choice is empowered, you can welcome anybody to join the gathering by sending the greeting join. In the event that the "mysterious join" work is

incapacitated, a virtual entryway is set up that requires meeting affirmation from the host. Groups likewise permits you to welcome individuals by their telephone number and email address. Utilize the "Welcome individuals" choice to welcome individuals before the gathering begins. Or on the other hand welcome individuals via looking through their names, email locations, or telephone numbers in the pursuit box, and afterward send invitations.

Meeting Controls

Administrators can handle different settings such as:

Audio Conferencing

If you have a sound conferencing permit, individuals can dial into your gatherings from more than 90 countries.

Virtual Lobby

People from outside your association will show up in a virtual entryway. This permits you more command over who can get to the discussion and who can't upon entry.

Mute

Mute noisy attendees during a meeting with the mute button  For large meetings the muting function is essential.

Screen Sharing

Easily share your screen during a meeting by clicking the centrally located up arrow screen button  . Once you click this button, Teams gives you the option to choose your entire desktop, a specific window, or files located on your computer.

Recording Calls

Microsoft Teams permits you to record gatherings. To begin a recording, click the three spots or More Options button and select Start Recording. When the

meeting is finished, a recording is sent to your inbox.

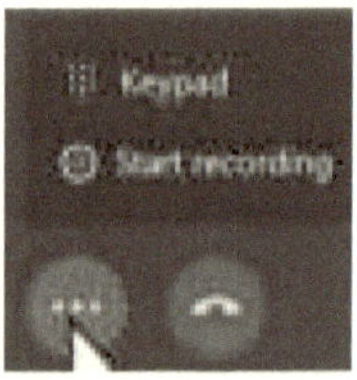

Zoom video conferencing integration with Microsoft Teams

MicroAll in allft Teams offers designers the capacity to fabricate reconciliations with non-Office 365 items. One of these incorporations is a Zoom Video conferencing module which empowers clients to send off Zoom gatherings from inside Teams. By utilizing Zoom with Teams, clients can use the advantages of Zoom straightforwardly inside Office 365. Anybody utilizing Office 365 approaches Microsoft Teams for video conferencing. So, you may ask why you would need to incorporate Zoom into your Teams climate? You'll find out with regards to Zoom video conferencing and its numerous interesting elements in the following chapter.

Enhancing Productivity

Increased usefulness is probably the best advantage of video conferencing. You might observe that a portion of the clients in your organization need more video conferencing highlights than Teams alone offers. For instance,

Zoom highlights online course answers for have gatherings for huge number of participants. Zoom additionally presents the capacity of facilitating bigger gatherings to 1,000 that include video specialists on screen. These are only a portion of the reasons that organizations might need to coordinate Zoom with Teams. The Zoom for Teams module is only one of the numerous reconciliations accessible for Teams users.

Conclusion

Microsoft Teams is a strong application that unites a large number of the main advantages of working on the web together into a solitary durable application. Microsoft's online work area spans customary well known applications with on-premise arrangements in the cloud-like not many organizations can. Microsoft's Office 365 and Microsoft Teams items together are changing the manner in which a large number of individuals work. In the following section, you'll find out with regards to Zoom video conferencing.

7 ZOOM VIDEO CONFERENCING

Topic/Feature:	Details:
Date Started	Founded in 2011 and launched in 2013
Price	Freemium Model puts a 40-minute limit on free users (unlimited 1:1 meetings). Paid plans range from $14.99-19.99.
Meeting Participants	Maximum of 100-300. Varies with a plan (Enterprise supports up to 1,000).
Estimated Monthly Users	300 Million
Breakout Rooms	Yes, paid users can host up to 50 breakout rooms which can be automatically or manually assigned.
Instant Messaging	Chat messaging available in-meetings and in-client
Unique Feature #1	The intuitive control bar is easy to use yet powerful.
Unique Feature #2	Robust security controls, updated after security flaw exposure in Q1 of 2020.

Zoom is one of the main suppliers of video conferencing programming. Only seven years later the organization's 2013 send off, Zoom has turned into the quickest developing web-based correspondences organization on the planet. With such countless elements, incorporating a visit connect with cross-stage informing and top tier video conferencing, many are going to Zoom as their best option to deal with their changing innovation needs.

Zoom's prominence accompanies valid justification first, they back their element rich stage with a group of amicable client assistance delegates. Eric Yuan the CEO of Zoom, has turned into an industry figured pioneer with a mission to "convey joy to clients." With all of that at the top of the priority list, Zoom's balanced stage has over and over been positioned number one in client surveys on

G2Crowd, TrustRadius, and Gartner Peer Insights, among other platforms.

The stage has a ton making it work, it's not difficult to utilize and very solid. Another champion element is its point of interaction which shows individuals in little "Brady Bunch" squares, conveniently fitting up to 49 individuals on a similar screen. The application is the thing that specialized financial backers call "tacky" which means clients get so joined to utilizing it, they'd never consider changing to another. In this part, you will get an inside and out investigate all that you want to know to be fruitful with Zoom.

Let's get started!

Zoom Overview

One glance at Zoom's site will let you know how well known the help is. Zoom has tributes from the absolute greatest undertakings on the planet, yet Zoom's not only for enormous name organizations, particularly following the pandemic of 2020 compelling everybody to telecommute. Zoom is currently utilized by little and enormous organizations the same, just as not-for-profits, legislatures, establishments, and people around the world, satisfying a steadily developing need for keeping individuals connected.

What Are the Main Zoom Services?

Zoom's principle administration is video correspondences. The connection point is basic enough for anybody to see how to involve it in only a couple of moments. The application configuration includes a video "up front" style approach with a solitary control bar on the bottom.

The Zoom meeting control bar highlights basic symbols that address the mouthpiece control, camera use, members, visit, screen sharing, recording, and response. Zoom keeps a shortsighted and natural connection point and a large number of these symbols drill down to get to more profound degrees of control. In the engine, Zoom offers numerous video conferencing highlights that its rivals don't. Hence, Zoom has turned into a top pick for power clients who host loads of internet based gatherings. Clients frequently pick Zoom for its considerable rundown of highlights, however the genuine magnificence of Zoom is its unwavering quality. Individuals love utilizing Zoom since its motivation assembled plan works for them 99.99% of the time with no requirement for IT support. The effortlessness of the plan causes clients to feel like they are in charge of their meetings.

Zoom's features include:

- Large Meetings: Support for up to 1,000 video members on up to 49 recordings on-screen at a time, all featuring HD sound and video.
- Screen Sharing: Zoom's screen sharing choices are coordinated into Basic, Advanced and Files tabs.
    - The Basic tab gives you choices to pick any screen on your PC with a possibility for whiteboards, iPhone/iPads, and any open window.
    - The Advanced tab gives admittance to choices to sharing

explicit areas of your screen, music just or an optional camera.

- The Files tab will permit you to share explicit documents from Microsoft OneDrive, Google Drive and Box.

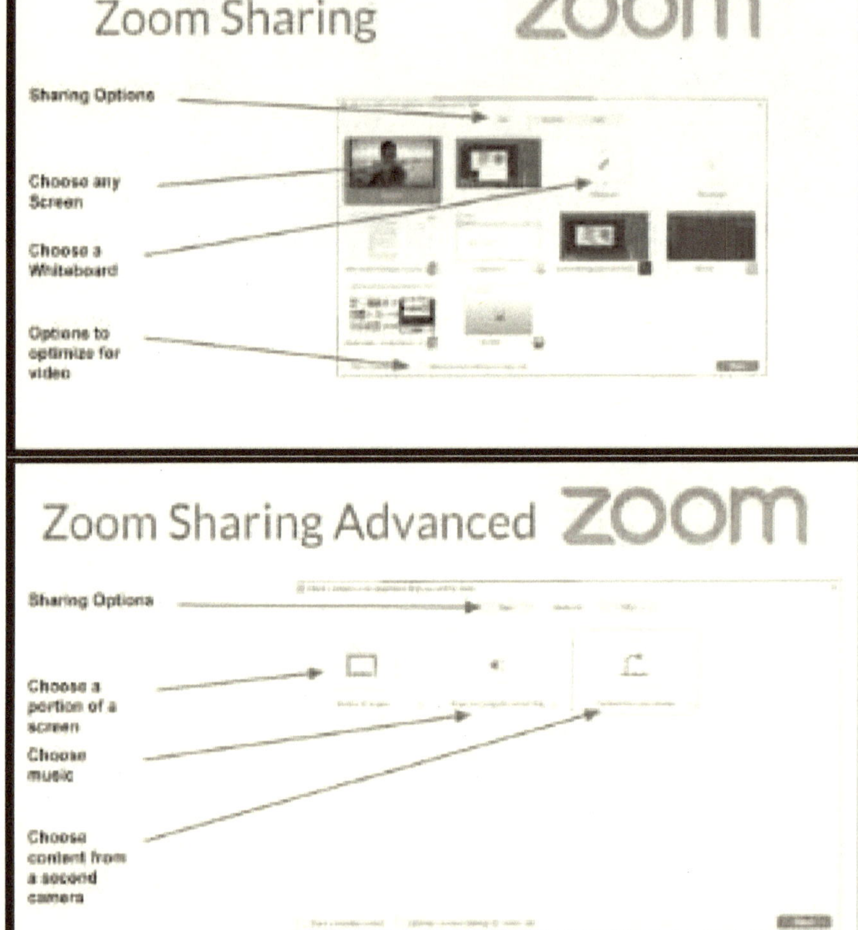

- Collaboration: Built-in cooperation instruments let members share screens and whiteboards. Comment devices add intelligence, so clients can make dynamic introductions and clarify archives with highlighters and advanced ink. Explanation apparatuses show at the highest point of the screen once a screen share meeting is in progress.

- Security: Zoom offers job based client security, secret word assurance, member holds, lounge areas, and encryption for each gathering. In 2020 another attention on security made Zoom 5.0 quite possibly the most dependable solution accessible. Zoom permits generally paid clients to choose where their information is steered with choices for choosing servers all over the planet. Then, a Security button on the gathering control board gives clients fast access highlights to lock gatherings, empower sitting areas, confine member screen sharing, talking, and renaming themselves. Other meeting security measures such as meeting passwords still need to be set up before the meeting starts.

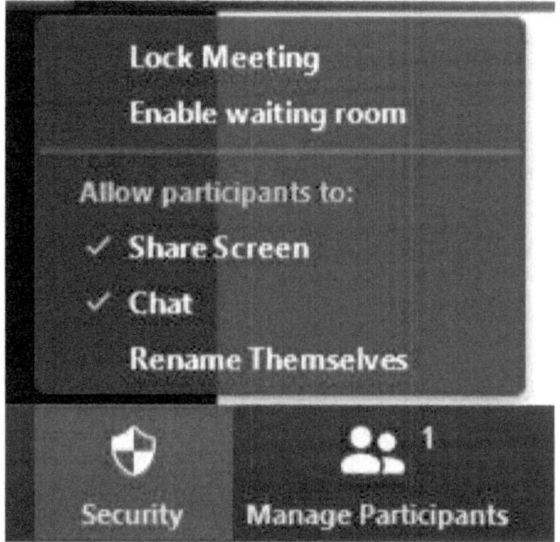

- Recordings: Meetings are effectively recorded and can be saved to the cloud or locally. Accounts saved in the cloud are referred to using

accessible records. Start a recording meeting by tapping the Record button and picking a capacity area. When recording, members see a red symbol on the upper left corner of the gathering window. The gathering host stops or closures the recording from the upper left of the screen or within the gathering control bar. Of course, recorded sound/video documents are changed over into .mp4 documents or the host can likewise decide to save sound just (.mp4).

- Calendars: Streamline booking and beginning of Zoom gatherings from other well known schedule stages with modules for iCal, Gmail, and Outlook.

Google Calendar Example

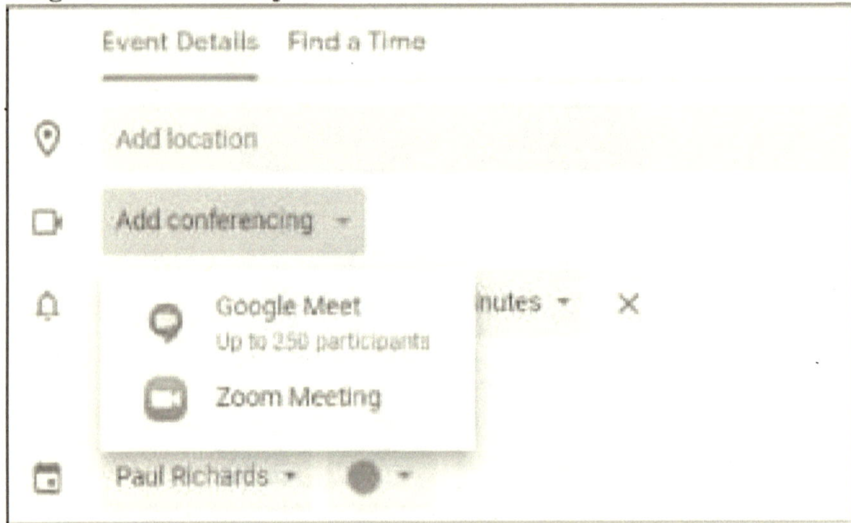

- Messaging: Team Chat allows gatherings to cooperate with accessible history, document sharing, and a 10-year file. Convert private talks into video calls with a tick of a button.
- Zoom Phone: Zoom telephone allows clients to overhaul a call to a gathering seamlessly.
- Breakout Rooms: Meeting hosts can sort out smaller than usual

gatherings inside bigger gatherings by tapping the Breakout Room button and choosing the quantity of rooms and regardless of whether to relegate members physically or automatically.

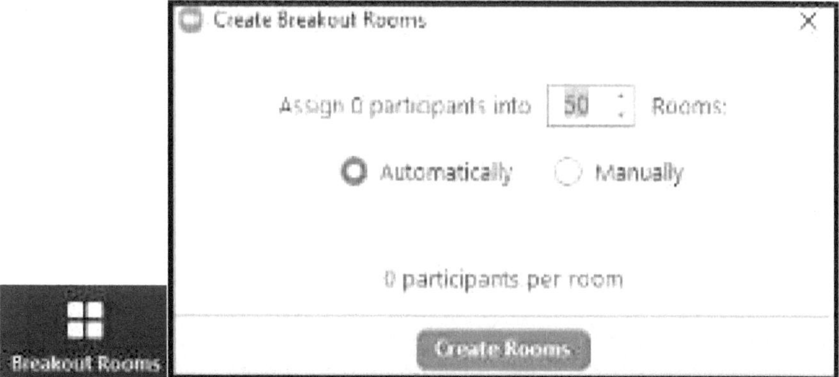

Using Breakout Rooms requires the board from a host. See the accompanying table for the momentum impediments of breakout rooms:

Number of breakout rooms	Max participants in the main meeting*	Max participants in each breakout room
20 breakout rooms	Up to 500 participants	25
30 breakout rooms	Up to 400 participants	13
50 breakout rooms	Up to 200 participants	4

*The huge gathering add-on is needed for gatherings with up to 500 participants.

Now that you're familiar with Zoom, we should take a nearer look.

Online Meetings

With Zoom, you can have online gatherings effortlessly or direct preparing and cooperative research organizations on one consistent stage. Zoom gatherings conveys endeavor video conferencing complete with content sharing and bound together communications.

The worked on connection point is accessible for use across any gadget which makes beginning and joining gatherings a breeze. Zoom likewise matches up with your schedule framework utilizing modules for Google Calendar and Microsoft Exchange. Zoom has also designed integrations for popular collaboration suites such as Microsoft

Video Webinars

Webinars are superb for creating drives, leading preparing inside an association, and in different applications. Zoom's office for online courses is like customary Zoom gatherings, however with added Q&A highlights for overseeing high participant limit. Zoom online classes let you have online occasions with up to 100 intuitive video members who can be overhauled from participant jobs to specialist jobs who offer admittance to sound and video controls.
Or, select a Zoom online course plan for up to 10,000 view-only attendees.

No matter the size of your online course, you'll partake in the simple set-up. When utilized for deals prospecting, Zoom incorporates with showcasing stages to upgrade the whole interaction. Enrolling is straightforward as well. You can tweak and brand your messages and enlistment structures to stream flawlessly with the remainder of your site or association. Adaptable devices like enrollment the executives and numerous joining choices guarantee Zoom associates easily with your CRM. Moreover, you can even adapt your online course involving PayPal incorporation with Zapier to oversee participant installment for your online course.

At the point when it comes time to introduce, Zoom's online class controls are both straightforward and instinctive. Zoom's presentation includes unique, multimedia options, to keep the audience engaged such as private and group chat settings for both attendees and panelists and an area for Q&A and polling with live or text- based answers.

A "hand-raising" highlight expands member commitment by permitting participants to call your consideration when they have questions. The Attention Indicator tracks how connected with your crowd is all through the online class and shows you which watchers are taking the most interest. Since Zoom incorporates with CRM arrangements like Salesforce, the Attention Indicator demonstrates really important for follow-up later the online class is complete.

Conference Rooms

"Zoom Rooms" takes video conferencing into the cutting edge time, with an encounter planned explicitly for internet meeting spaces. With regards to convenience, Zoom Rooms handles the three greatest obstacles individuals face with virtual gathering rooms: booking and beginning a gathering, and sharing substance. With Zoom's standard features, such as HD video and audio, video conferences go off without a hitch, but Zoom Rooms takes things even further.

Zoom Rooms is intended to give a control framework to your meeting room with "One-contact" on a gadget like an iPad, where one-contact join highlight makes getting into a gathering really straightforward, Furthermore a single tick remote offer makes content sharing simple. And, with regards to appointments, schedule combinations with Exchange, Google Calendar, or Office 365 methods members will not be looking for meeting login details.

To help joint effort, members can open up to 12 whiteboards at a time with annotation apparatuses to assist them with cooperating. Co-explanation added across work area and cell phones is put away and can be shared for future reference. At no extra expense, Zoom Rooms additionally gives advanced signage and a planning show. Also, you can work on your room arrangement and with far off administration, programming provisioning, area orders, job based organization, and alerts...ultimately decreasing your IT costs.

Zoom Phone

Global availability...from anyplace is conceivable utilizing Zoom. Zoom Phone is an endeavor cloud-based telephone framework that improves your customary telephone framework with extra highlights for smoothed out client experience. Presently, raising a call to a video meeting should be possible with the snap of a button.

Managing clients, astutely observing business connections, and rapidly provisioning assets is completely simplified on account of an instinctive and unified Admin gateway. Besides, Zoom Phone is profoundly solid and secure, offering excellent worldwide conveyance of HD Voice.

Zoom tries to be the one brought together stage that can deal with an entire set-up of business obligations. Zoom Phone expands these capacities. Settle on and

get decisions flawlessly while partaking in video gatherings, sending visit messages, sharing substance, and more with Zoom's portable and work area applications. Convert calls to Zoom Meetings without hanging up. Auto chaperons and clever call steering settle on certain decisions are associated safely and never missed. Advantageous mixes with Microsoft Office 365, Google G-Suite, Salesforce, and others let clients experience Zoom while as yet utilizing their most loved applications.

Zoom Phone additionally includes mail and call recording to permit you to rapidly get to interpreted messages or calls from any of your gadgets. Zoom Phone upholds your present public exchanged phone organization (PSTN) specialist co-op from anyplace on the planet. Zoom Phone likewise upholds VoIP gadgets like those from Yealink and Polycom, among others.

Zoom Chat

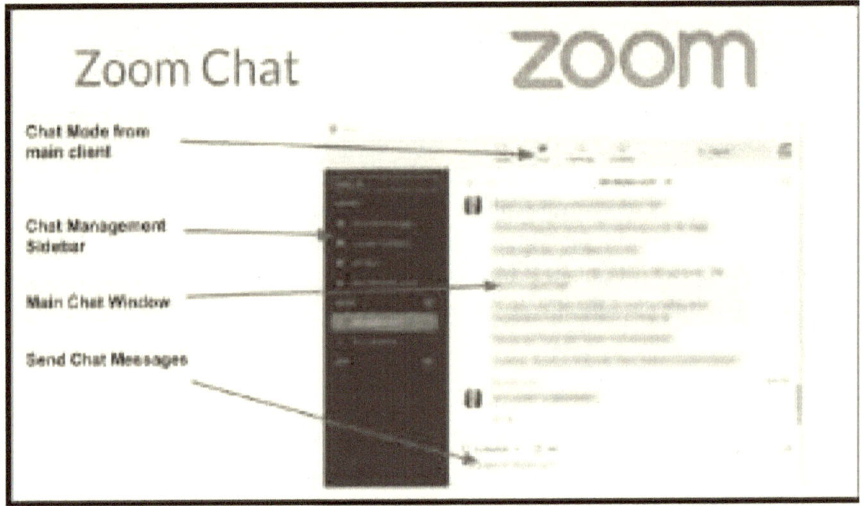

Subscribe to any Zoom plan and Zoom Chat is incorporated with your permit. Zoom Chat incorporates directly into gatherings, online courses, and different apparatuses inside the Zoom stage. Knowing how to utilize Zoom Chat makes coordinated effort simpler than at any other time, regardless of whether talking among groups in your association or acquiring outside participants.

With Zoom, record sharing, taking screen captures, utilizing emoticons, and searching

across contacts, documents, and messages is all conceivable. Schedule combinations sync with contact status to demonstrate who's occupied and who's accessible (or not), regardless of which gadget they're on; whether work area or versatile, when they're on or disconnected - and that is only the beginning.

With Zoom Chat, you can make a virtual work area and add whoever might seem most appropriate for your activities. Empowering document sharing and coordinated correspondences with no of the turmoil related with most web visits. Remain fixed on the secret sauce by featuring your channels and contacts, alter your warnings to restrict interruptions, and coordinate what's vital to you.

How about having the option to start a gathering video from inside a channel or beginning a one-on-one gathering with anybody in a visit bunch. Consider the possibility that the gathering could even increase to 1,000 individuals; each outfitted with screen sharing and crisp and clean, sound/video abilities. To begin a Zoom visit you should simply add contacts to the talk region. Whenever you have contacts, off you go.

Wouldn't it be extraordinary to have the option to scan messages for content and connections? Zoom has that. A 10-year message chronicling highlight forestalls incidental cancellations. All of this and you can likewise be sure with regards to security realizing that Zoom scrambles every one of the information constantly and watches the entryways with SSO and multifaceted authentication.

Let's Get You Started with Zoom

Because it's so highlight rich, numerous new clients are scared by Zoom. Zoom brings together gathering informing, online gatherings, and cloud conferencing into one device. Be that as it may, while so exceptionally practical, Zoom stays natural and easy to utilize, regardless of whether you're on a Windows, Mac, or Chromium Device. Here are the means to follow to kick off Zoom:

Sign In

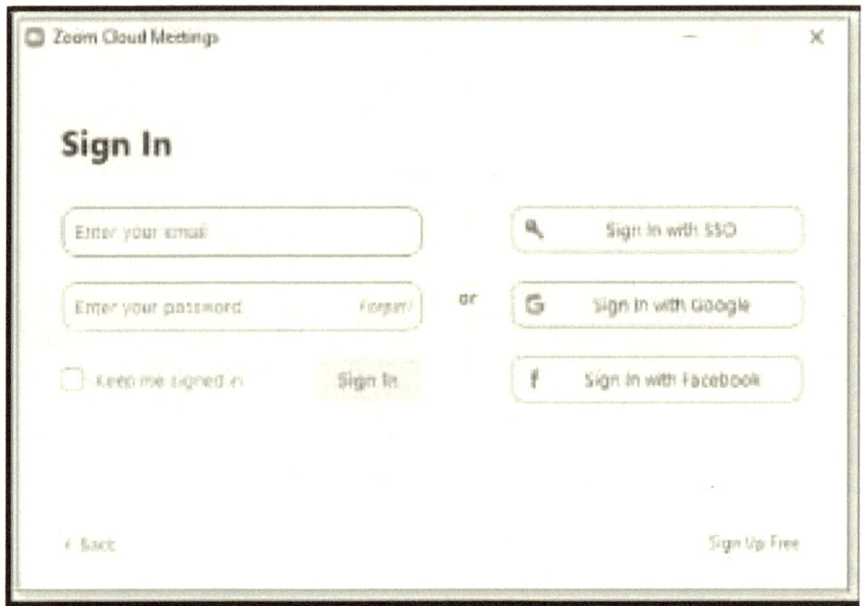

After introducing the Zoom work area customer for your gadget, you really want to sign in. Indeed, you can join a gathering without marking in, with accreditations gave in a gathering, yet to begin or timetable your gathering you should sign in.

Sign in choices incorporate, utilizing Zoom, Google, or Facebook qualifications relying upon how you set your record up. You can likewise utilize SSO (Single Sign-On). Assuming you haven't set up a Zoom account, click Sign Up Free. Assuming you've failed to remember your secret word, click Forgot to reset it.

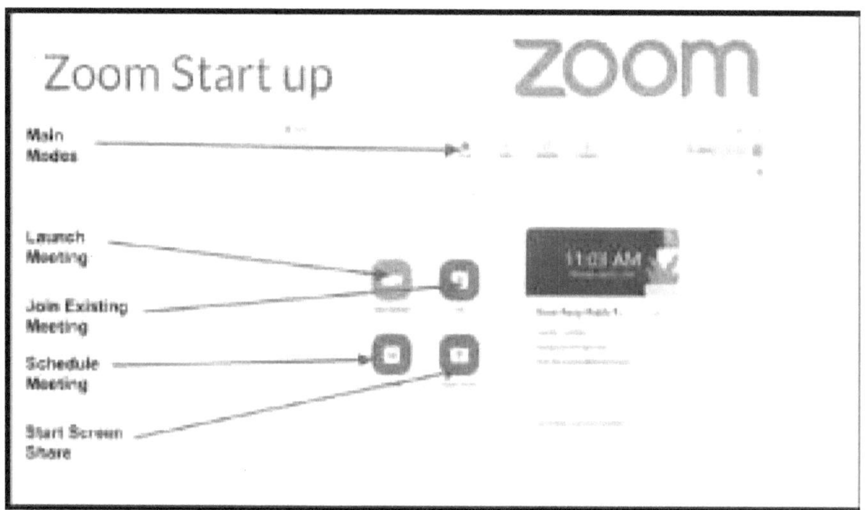

Home

Once you've endorsed into your record, the Home tab shows with the following:

- New Meeting: Instantly start another gathering with or without video. Click the down bolt to empower video or use your PMI (Personal Meeting ID) to make a moment meeting.
- Join: Join a gathering that is effectively in the works or currently planned with a Meeting ID.
- Schedule: Schedule a future meeting.
- Share Screen: Share your screen in a Zoom Room; with your sharing key or a gathering ID.
- Upcoming Meeting: Indicates the following gathering set for the current day. Add an outsider schedule to match up with your record to see all of your impending meetings.

One of the coolest choices in Zoom is the capacity to change your experience picture. Simply float over the image and snap on the camera symbol to change it.

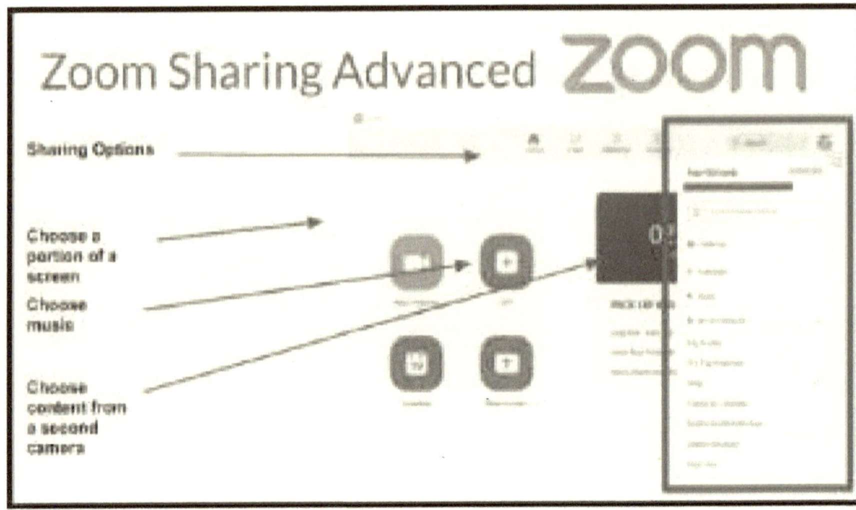

To investigate extra choices, click on your profile picture for the accompanying features:

- Add an individual note.
- Change your status to Away, Do Not Disturb, or Available.
- Upgrade to Pro (if utilizing a free account).
- Sign Out of your account.
- Switch to Portrait View for a smaller window.
- Use Chat, to see your private discussions with contacts or channels.
- Use Settings to change and refresh settings in the client.
- View My Profile tab, you can open the online interface to alter your profile.
- Access Help, for help from the Zoom Help Center.
- Check for Updates to guarantee you've the most recent rendition of the Zoom work area client.

A left side board on the principle Zoom dashboard will open for admittance to new highlights contingent upon which tab you are right now on. The tabs incorporate Home, Chat, Meetings and Contacts.

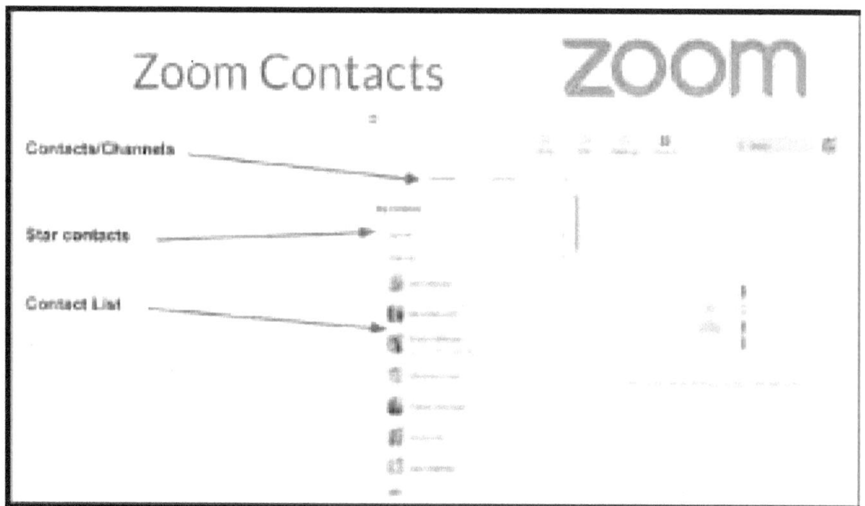

The Contacts tabs is an incredible instrument for adding your kin to Zoom. Select a contact or channel from the left side board for the following:

1. Star: Star a contact or channel for speedy access.
2. Video: Click the video symbol to start a gathering with a chose contact, or channel (to welcome every one of its individuals to your meeting).
3. New Window: Hover over a contact or channel name to see and snap a symbol to open the visit in a new window.
4. Info: Additional choices for the chose contact or channel with fast admittance to featured messages, pictures, and records inside the chat.
5. Message box: Sends a message to your contact or channel alongside code pieces, GIFs, screen captures, or files.
6. Phone: Select the Phone tab to start a call, view call history, or send phone message informing with the Zoom Phone. Note: A Zoom Phone permit is needed to do so.

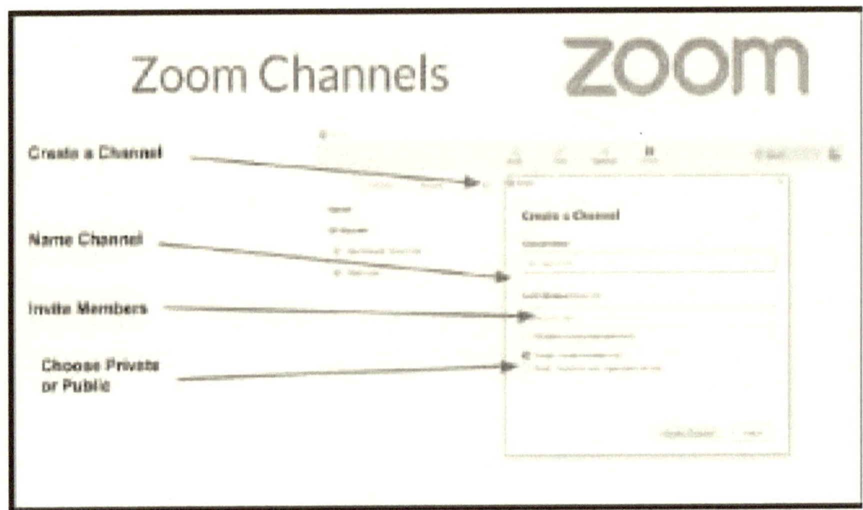

Create channels for coordinated effort. Channels assist you with following gathering projects and are a spot to save discussions which can become video gatherings. To begin another channel, click the in addition to fasten close to Channels and finish up the subtleties. Unveiling a divert permits anybody in your association to join. Notice each contact has a status symbol before their name, informing you as to whether they're accessible or not.

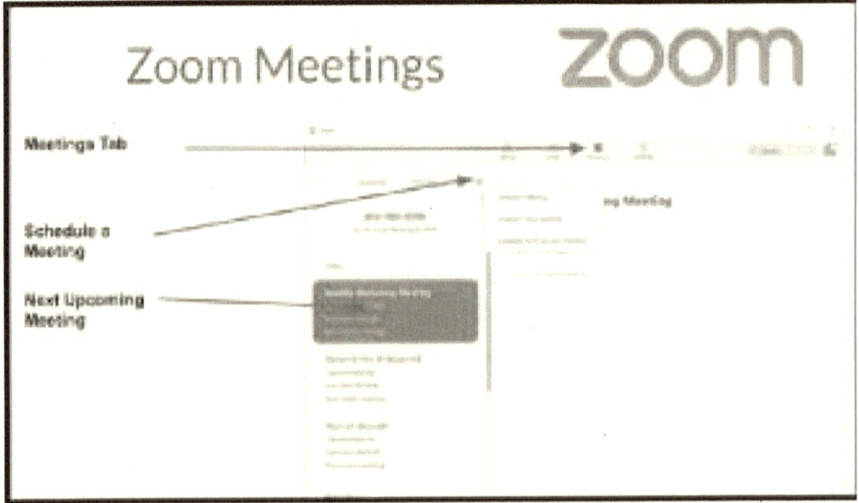

Meetings

After looking into the Zoom dashboard, it's an ideal opportunity to make a beeline for the Meetings tab. This is the spot to see, start, alter, and erase booked meetings.

Select a planned gathering to these choices in the left side panel:

- Add: Click to plan a new meeting.
- Refresh: Click to invigorate the gathering list not seeing a booked meeting.
- Start: Click to begin the booked gathering selected.
- Copy Invitation: Copy the greeting text from a gathering and glue it into an email or moment messenger.
- Edit: Edit the choices for your planned meeting.
- Delete: Permanently erase the booked meeting.

Scheduling Zoom Meetings

Starting a Zoom meeting is however kind with the spot as it very well might be ahead of time. Planning for advance allows you to more readily oversee choices and builds security by means of discretionary settings like Recurring, accommodating for week by week registrations or classes when meets simultaneously consistently.

Whether you're utilizing the work area application, site, or even your portable application, the interaction is very

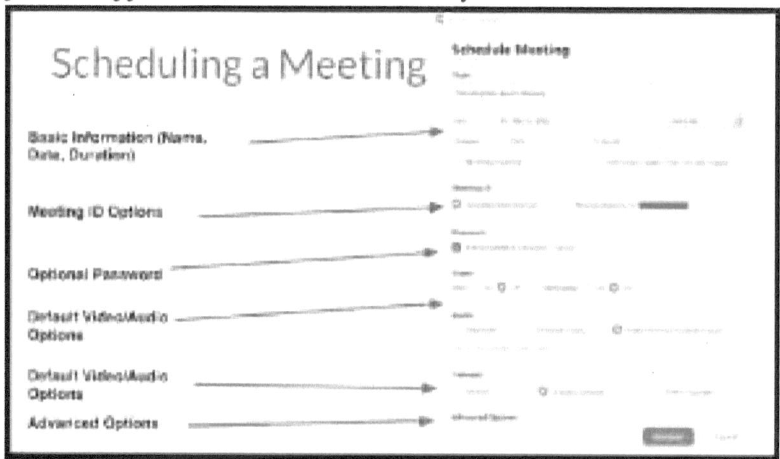

Schedule a Meeting from Your Desktop

The means to follow to plan a gathering from your work area is a similar whether involving Zoom in your internet browser or through a work area client.

On the Zoom.us website:

1. Click the **Meetings** tab in the Zoom dashboard then click the + (plus) button. Optionally you can click the **Schedule** button directly from the Zoom dashboard. 

2. A structure opens. Fill in the gathering subtleties, including a date and time. Pick aRecurring meeting or a one-time meeting. Finish up the entirety of the data and snap Save at the base when done.
3. For security consider adding a gathering secret key. Additionally, think about a portion of the Advanced choices that can expand your gathering experience.

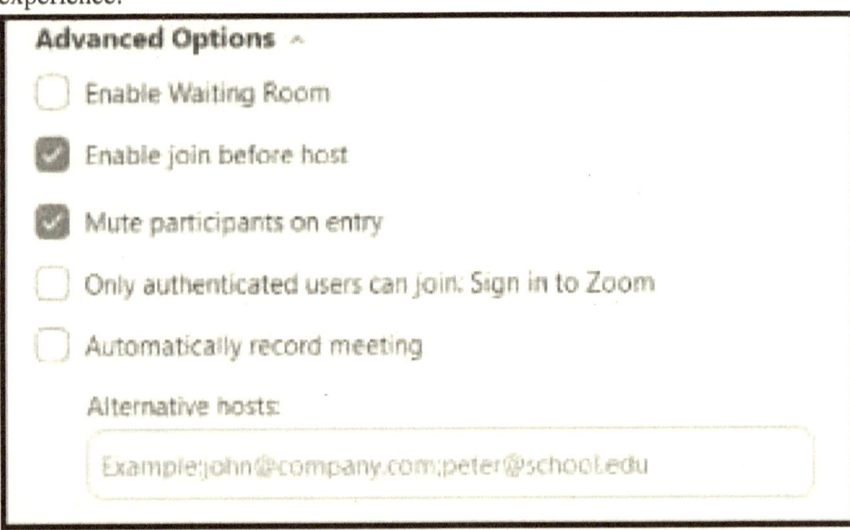

The lounge area include puts new gathering participants into a lounge area region where they delay until physically conceded into the gathering. You can empower a choice to permit members to join the gathering before the host, quiet members upon section, and naturally record the meeting.

Personal Meeting Rooms

Your Meeting ID (PMI) is a static gathering ID used to have gatherings with individuals you trust. It's vital to watch your PMI in light of the fact that any individual who has it can join your gatherings. You'll utilize the PMI when beginning or booking gatherings. PMI's are great for partaking in your email signature. An ideal illustration of the PMI is the point at which an educator utilizes a similar PMI every week to meet with understudies for night-time instructing meetings. The number is safely divided among understudies, and utilized for convenience.

Every Zoom client is additionally appointed a Personal Meeting Room. One helpful hint to make this gathering ID number essential is to utilize your 10-digit telephone number. This individual gathering room is a virtual space, got to with your

PMI. Your Personal Meeting Room PMI is great for consecutive gatherings assuming that the sitting area highlight is empowered. Thusly, you stay in one focal Zoom space without opening and restart each new gathering. With the sitting area include empowered, proceed with a current gathering and let your next gathering participant enter when you're ready.

If you give somebody your PMI interface, they can add someone else, except if you lock the gathering or utilize the Waiting Room. Empower "Join Before Host" to permit meeting participants to join the room before you arrive. As you can envision, openly given PMIs can make a few issues and it's probably the greatest slip-up new Zoom clients make when arranging public or gathering meetings.
Share your PMI with a lot of individuals or even via web-based media... also out of nowhere anybody with that connection can attack their Meeting Room.

We'll delve into this all the more later on when we investigate how to control admittance to your gatherings. Until further notice, what you really want to know is the way to utilize your PMI when it's fitting to do as such. A great many people select a setting to utilize their PMI to begin moment gatherings. The other choice is to allow Zoom to produce an arbitrary ID. Set Zoom to always use your PMI for instant start meetings, in the Zoom web portal by clicking on your profile photo then clicking Edit next to your Meeting ID and checking Use this ID for instant meetings.

Save your progressions and you're done.

What Not to Do with Your PMI

Zoom is an adaptable instrument that has acquired huge prevalence as the world interest for great video meeting apparatuses has developed. One especially fun use case for Zoom is "public occasions" and enormous gatherings with outside visitors. Public occasions welcome a wide range of individuals to join a cordial discussion, watch a film, jam music, or simply share about anything possible. In the realm of business, public occasions are additionally extremely valuable as an instrument for building interest among likely customers by welcoming them to a live direction or online course type occasion. While facilitating public occasions, notwithstanding, be aware of how you set up the invitations.

Ideally, don't your PMI for such occasions in light of the fact that an excessive number of individuals will wind up having your PMI assuming you do. All things being equal, utilize the choice to produce an irregular gathering ID. It's best practice to utilize an irregular ID when:

- Sharing your PMI on friendly media.
- You aren't yet mindful of the accepted procedures of Zoom privacy
- You don't anticipate meeting consistently

Fortunately, utilizing an arbitrary gathering ID is

easy. Producing a Random Meeting ID

When setting up a gathering, pick Meeting ID and Generate Automatically or to utilize your PMI. Regardless, you can require a gathering secret phrase as an additional a stage of safety to restrict who might join. We will survey data about gathering passwords and "two-factor validation" a piece later.

Inviting Meeting Participants

Whether beginning a moment meeting or booking one, there are a few techniques to browse to welcome members. Assuming that you download the Cloud Room Connector add-on, you will actually want to welcome a room system.
Additionally, you can welcome by telephone in the event that you have a sound conferencing plan. Without these extra additional items, you can in any case utilize the accompanying options.

Instant Meeting Invites

To begin a moment meeting click Manage Participants at the lower part of the window, select Invite on the board of members, and browse the accompanying options:

Email

Email is a fast and simple choice, select the Invite by Email tab and pick an email supplier. The default utilizes the email application on your PC. Then again, you can utilize Google or Yahoo Mail, which will provoke you to sign into your email account.

An email is created consequently, and all of the gathering data is set in the body of the email. Simply add the beneficiaries and send it out.

Contacts

Click the Manage Participants choice and go to Invite at the lower part of the board of members. Click the Invite by Contacts tab and select the contact's name from the window. You can likewise look for a particular contact.

Click on an individual and their names show a mark close to them. They are additionally added to the rundown at the highest point of the window. Click Invite in the lower right corner to send the solicitations to the chose contacts.

URL / Invitation Text

You can click Copy URL or Copy Invitation to send moment meeting information anyplace you wish. Duplicate the gathering join connect for simple sharing or duplicate the full greeting to clarify the gathering's subtleties close by the greeting join. Right-click and select Paste or use Ctrl + V on Windows or Cmd + V on a Mac.

Scheduled Meeting Invites

Once you plan a gathering, you can start welcoming members. On the work area customer, in the wake of booking, go to your Meetings tab. Select the gathering you need to welcome members to and afterward click Copy Invitation. This duplicates the gathering greeting so you can glue it anyplace, as into an email or onto an online media page.

Through the web-based interface, sign in and click Meetings. Click on the subject of the gathering and, close to Time, you'll see choices for adding the gathering to your calendar.

If you select Yahoo Calendar or Google Calendar, it will consequently make an occasion in your schedule adjusted with the email administration you pick. Click Outlook Calendar to produce a .ics record you can bring into your Calendar.

You can likewise physically duplicate the greeting. Another window opens with the gathering greeting text. Click Select All in this window, duplicate it, and afterward send it through email or chat.

Joining a Test Meeting

Use Test gatherings to evaluate your arrangement and get familiar with Zoom before you're put on a spot in a genuine gathering. While Zoom is natural and simple to utilize, it's positively beneficial to attempt a test meeting once, particularly to turn into a Zoom Pro!

Joining a test meeting is simple. On a mobile device, visit http://zoom.us/test and follow the instructions shown to test your video or audio. Otherwise, visit http://zoom.us/test on your desktop and click the blue Join button.

The program will provoke you to "Open Zoom Meetings." If you don't have the work area customer introduced, follow the prompts. At the point when the work area customer is open, a test meeting shows in a spring up window. This is the place where to test your speakers for sound result by tapping the Test Audio button. Assuming you don't hear a ringtone make light of utilization the drop menu to switch your speaker selection.

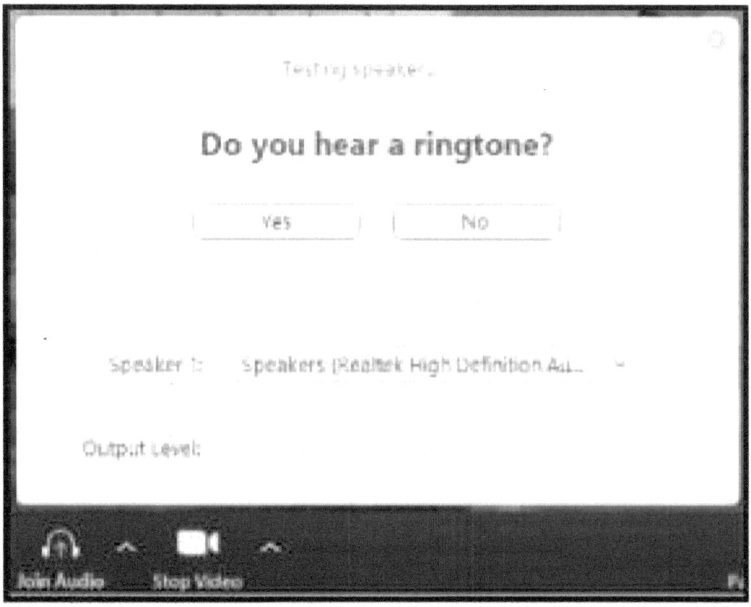

When you hear the ringtone play, click Yes, and proceed with the amplifier test. At the point when your amplifier is working, you'll hear sound replay through your speakers. On the off chance that you don't hear an answer, click No to switch mouthpieces and rehash the interaction until you hear the replay. Click Yes when you hear the replay.

The following thing to do is click Join with Computer Audio to join the test meeting with the amplifier and speakers you recently tried. You will presently be a participant of the test meeting. This is a fantastic chance to learn about

how participants see your video feed and to become accustomed to a portion of the controls.

Obviously, your arrangement probably won't be wonderful from the start. In the following area, we'll plunge into the subtleties for setting up your sound and video for amazing real time. Then we'll look at screen sharing and some other features you'll want to take advantage of as you become a Zoom Pro.

Preparing Your Audio

Always test your sound before a gathering. To really look at your PC's sound, click on the bolt close to the quiet symbol. This opens up a rundown of Audio choices where you can choose Test Computer Audio to test your speakers and microphone.

The test will give you the important prompts to finish. At the point when gotten done, just close the testing window. Zoom works with outer speakers and receivers alongside headsets.

A straightforward method for ensuring your mouthpiece is working is to search for the green "levels" that showcase within the amplifier symbol on the lower left of the screen. If a red strike is showing up through the microphone icon, then you are currently muted. Unmute by tapping on the receiver symbol.

Using Push to Talk

Zoom is loaded up with highlights that assist with making joining in and running gatherings a breeze, and "Push to Talk" is one element that assists you with staying away from undesirable prattle while ensuring everybody has a simple, advantageous conferencing experience.

Enable the Push To talk element to abstain from continually quieting or unmuting. To empower it in the work area customer, click on your profile picture and afterward go to Settings. Click the Audio tab and actually look at the choice to "Press and hold SPACE key to briefly unmute yourself." Save your settings. With this empowered, you will be quieted of course. To talk, you simply hold down the space bar.

Troubleshooting Issues

A sound reverberation is one of the most widely recognized sound issues to investigate. A reverberation is for the most part because of one of three things:

- Having both PC and phone sound active
- Having a PC or phone speakers excessively near each other
- Having various PCs with dynamic sound inside the equivalent room

There can likewise be sound impedance from a terrible receiver, speakers being excessively clearly, or a reverberation scratch-off disappointment (which is a gadget execution issue). As a host, you can quiet a participant to quietness the issue or quiet everybody to guarantee no impedance. The participant can likewise quiet themselves until they figure out the issue.

Preparing Your Video

A test meeting can test your video. Nonetheless, past guaranteeing your camera is dynamic, there are additionally another subtleties and settings you probably will need to address.

Rotate Your Camera

For Windows clients, the camera might show topsy turvy or sideways. To fix this, pivot the camera in your settings area until it's accurately oriented.

If you observe this is an issue before a gathering begins, sign in to your Zoom customer, click your profile picture, go to Settings and afterward the Video tab, float over your camera's review, and snap Rotate 90° until it's arranged correctly.

If you're in a gathering and notice that you want to turn your camera, click the bolt close to Stop Video and pick Video Settings, drift over your camera's see, and pivot the camera with the Rotate 90° button until it's situated correctly.

Use A Virtual Background

Virtual foundations permit you to change the setting behind you, which can unquestionably be entertaining. This element works best with lighting and a green screen behind you. The strong green tone from a green screen assists Zoom with recognizing you and your environmental factors. Be that as it may, a strong divider will likewise work. Utilizing a virtual foundation is direct and easy to set up.

You'll get the best outcomes if you:

- Use a strong foundation tone, ideally green.
- Use a HD webcam.
- Use uniform lighting all through your space.
- Do not wear clothing that matches your experience or virtual background.
- Use a foundation picture with a perspective proportion of 16:9 and a base goal of 1280 by 720 or utilize a video with a base goal of 360p and a most extreme goal of 1080p.

To empower a Virtual Background, sign into the Zoom online interface, and go to My Meeting Settings or Meeting Settings. Explore to the Virtual Background choice in the Meeting tab and confirm its empowered. Assuming that it's handicapped, flip the Status to empower it. Assuming that a confirmation discourse springs up, click Turn On.

If the choice is turned gray out, Virtual Backgrounds might be locked out at the Group or Account level, which implies you want to contact your Zoom administrator.

For the setting to produce results, log out of the Zoom Desktop Client and afterward log back in once more. Inside the work area customer, click on your profile picture and go to Settings. Select Virtual Background and check whether or not you have a green screen. Pick a picture to use as your background.

You might have to download the "Savvy Virtual Background" bundle to utilize a virtual foundation without a green screen. You'll just have to do this once.
To enable it just click the ^ next to Start/Stop Video and select Choose a Virtual Background.

Touch Up My Appearance

The "Final detail My Appearance" choice puts a delicate spotlight on your video show, assisting with introducing a more cleaned look before sun-down out your complexion on screen. To enact this, login to your Zoom customer, go to Settings, and afterward Video. Then again, during a gathering, click the bolt close to the video symbol and pick Video Settings.

Once you're in the settings exchange, click Touch Up My Appearance and really look at the choice to start showing cleaned up video. Zoom will recall your inclinations for future gatherings, so it will remain dynamic until you turn it off.

Screen Sharing

Share your screen in a gathering by tapping the green Share Screen symbol in the focal point of the base control bar. While a host doesn't have to allow participant to share their screen, they can keep participants from screen sharing by changing their settings. Here are some different choices you might need to investigate with regards to screen sharing.

Side-by-Side View

When screen sharing, members can change to next to each other mode, which permits them to see both the screen being shared and the Speaker View or Gallery View of members. In next to each other mode, you can change a separator between the common screen and video stream(s).

When viewing a screen in a meeting, click Options then select Side-by-Side Mode to enter this Split Screen. The common screen shows on the left and the speaker(s) on the right. To leave next to each other mode, return to Options and uncheck it. The screen being imparted assumes control over the window to the speaker(s) displayed along the top.

Annotations

Annotation devices are incredibly useful for hosts and members, yet the principal thing you really want to do is change your settings to empower explanations. As a host, you're in charge and can turn comment abilities on or off for the participants.

When sharing your screen or opening a whiteboard, you'll see the explanation controls spring up. Assuming they don't, select View Options and afterward select Annotate.

Note that the Select, Spotlight, and Save choices are simply accessible to the individual sharing the screen or whiteboard. Watchers won't see those choices. The following is a depiction of every comment apparatus and option:

- Mouse:Turn off comment devices and redisplay your mouse pointer by tapping the Mouse button. It's blue when you're utilizing your mouse pointer and the comment instruments are off.
- Select: Use this choice to choose, move, or resize comments. Select a few comments by clicking and hauling your mouse over them.
- Text: Insert text onto the screen or whiteboard.
- Draw: Inset lines, bolts, or shapes onto the screen or whiteboard.
- Note: Use this to feature a space of the common screen or whiteboard with a cloudy square or circle.
- Stamp: Insert predefined symbols, similar to a star or check mark.
- Spotlight/Arrow: Turn your cursor into a bolt or spotlight.
- Spotlight: Display your mouse pointer to members when sharing your screen or whiteboard to highlight things you need members to focus to.

- Arrow: Display a little bolt instead of your mouse pointer. Snap to embed a bolt that shows your name close to it. Click elsewhere to eliminate the last bolt you placed.
- Eraser: Click and haul to delete annotations.
- Format: Change the organizing choices for your devices, including line width, textual style, and color.
- Undo: Undo the last annotation.
- Redo: Redo the last comment that you undid.
- Clear: Remove all comments from the screen or whiteboard.
- Save: Save all comments as a screenshot.

Use a Watermark

When sharing your screen, select the Watermark element to superimpose a picture onto the common substance and the video of the individual sharing the substance. Start by signing into the Zoom online interface. Select Account and afterward Account Settings and track down the Add watermark choice in the Meeting tab to ensure the setting is enabled.

To utilize a Watermark, plan a gathering. Go to Meeting Options and empower the Enable watermark when seeing the common screen choice. In the event that you don't see these choices or you're not ready to initiate them, you'll have to ask your

Zoom Administrator to roll out the improvements for you.

With the Watermark, when a member shares their screen during the gathering, a piece of the email address of the individual survey the substance is forced on the common substance just as over the dynamic speaker's video. For instance, if someone with email testing@myzoommeeting.com is viewing shared content, the word Testing is forced over the video.

Zoom Meeting Controls

There are a few controls you ought to find out more about to utilize Zoom viably. Start by learning the fundamental controls prior to taking a gander at a portion of the more significant progressed choices you can utilize.

Basic Controls

When taking part in or running a Zoom meeting, you'll see various choices inside the Zoom window. Here is a glance at how you can manage them.

- Mute or Unmute Microphone: Control sound; when others in the meeting can hear you.
- Start or Stop Video: This setting permits you to begin or stop your video catch yet permits you to stay in a gathering as sound only.
- Change View: Use this choice to change your video show layout.
- Speaker: This choice allows you to see video of the dynamic speaker.
- Thumbnail: This choice allows you to show the video of the dynamic speaker with other participants' recordings showed in thumbnails beneath the dynamic speaker.
- Gallery: The showcase of each gathering participant in a grid.
- Camera Control: Use this to change the PTZ camera settings and presets or to change to an alternate camera. This component is empowered by a director. To control the PTZ camera on the furthest finish of a video call, demand camera control by right clicking a member's video.
- Participants/Manage Participants: View meeting members. The host consistently oversees participants.
- Invite: Invite Zoom contacts here or welcome them utilizing the email, telephone, or room system.

- Start Recording: Start recording to the cloud or your neighborhood drive.
- Settings: Use the room password to get to room settings.
- Volume Slider: Adjust the volume of the room's speaker. This resets to default toward the finish of each meeting.

The Zoom fundamental controls are utilized most frequently and genuinely simple. There are likewise best in class controls.

Advanced Controls

As with any open social affair, virtual gatherings require progressed controls for swarm the executives. Regardless of whether its people upsetting the occasion or performances who figured out how to find a welcome not planned for them, Zoom stars should know how to deal with intrusions.

Manage Screen Sharing

Perhaps the greatest slip-up new Zoom has make is delivering control of their screen. Never given an obscure individual access a public occasion take over your

screen or you might wind up imparting undesirable substance to everybody in the gathering. Continuously limit screen sharing previously and during the gathering with the host control bar. Select the choice to just permit the host to share their screen during a public meeting

Find have controls at the lower part of the window and snap the bolt close to Share Screen. Under Advanced Sharing Options, change Who can share to Only Host. In your web settings, you can likewise lock the Screen Share settings to Only Host naturally for all of your meetings.

Manage Your Participants

Zoom choices for public occasions let you have with full certainty. For example, you can select to confine occasions so that main endorsed in Zoom clients can join. At the point when a member requests to join and they aren't signed into Zoom, they'll see a login brief. The Authorized Attendees setting is one more method for controlling your visitor list.

Hosts can lock gatherings later every one of the approved members have joined. Consider this locking your gathering's front entryway. With a gathering locked, no other person can join, even with a gathering ID and secret phrase. To lock a meeting, click Participants at the bottom of your window then click the Lock Meeting button.

To eliminate undesirable members during a gathering, utilize the Participants' menu. Drift over a member's name and snap Remove to show them out of a gathering. Flip the setting to permit them back in the event that you unintentionally eliminate some unacceptable person.

Place a participant's video and sound associations on hold to briefly handicap them by clicking a member's video thumbnail and choosing Start Attendee On Hold to actuate. You can take them off hold when you are prepared to have them take an interest again.

You can comparably impair somebody's video or quiet them. Members can be quieted individually, or at the same time. Quiet Upon Entry is valuable to stay away from fuss in, especially huge gatherings. Select whether or not you need participants to have the option to unmute themselves. For enormous public gatherings, it's useful to have a co-host to assist you with overseeing who gets un-quieted utilizing the lift hand include. Make any gathering participant a co-have by giving them extra meeting control capacities from the Participants tab.

Hosting a Breakout Session

A breakout room allows you to part a Zoom getting into together to 50 separate meetings. The host of the gathering can decide to divide members into discrete meetings physically or naturally and can switch clients between meetings whenever. This is an extraordinary element for permitting little groups inside a bigger gathering to have explicit discussions outside of the primary video conference.

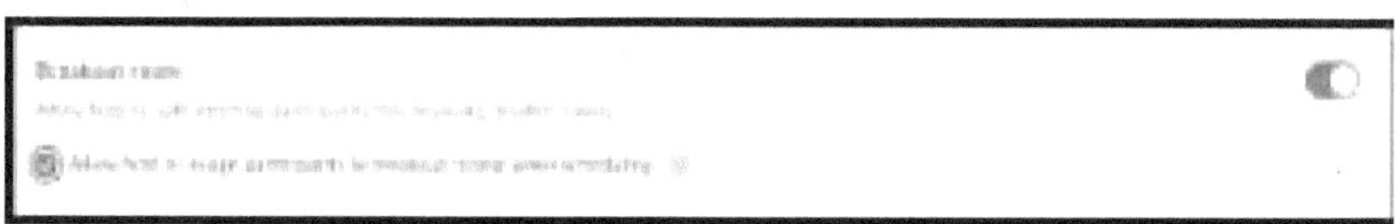

The Zoom Administrator of your record needs to empower Breakout Sessions for clients to get to this element. Once empowered, meeting hosts can empower or debilitate this from the Breakout Room button that showcases. Meeting hosts can relegate members to explicit breakout rooms or make members co-has who can move in the middle of breakout meetings themselves.

When overseeing breakout rooms, a significant hint is to pre-dole out clients to explicit rooms when planning the gathering. On the other hand, set things up so clients are doled out consequently. Understand that clients inside a lounge have full sound, video, and screen sharing capabilities.

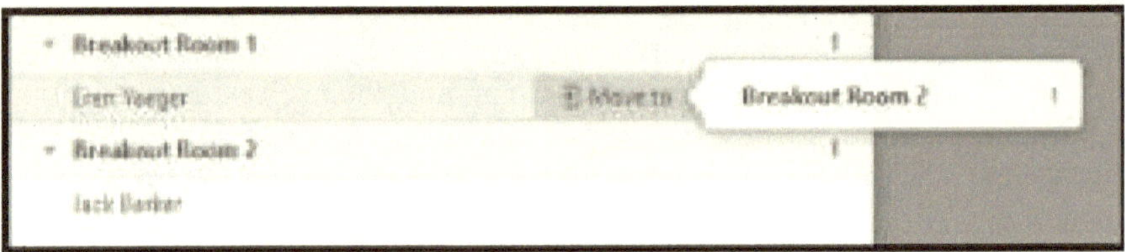

You can set up the accompanying choices for your breakout rooms.

- Automatically move members into breakout rooms. Really take a look at this choice to naturally move members into breakout rooms. Without checking it, members need to click Join to be added to a breakout room.
- Allow members to get back to the primary meeting whenever. Really take a look at this choice so members can decide to move back to the primary meeting with their gathering controls. Assuming you don't check it, they should trust that the host will end breakout spaces for everyone.
- Breakout rooms close consequently later X minutes. On the off chance that you check this choice, breakout rooms consequently end when the predetermined time is up.
- Notify me when the time is up. Check this choice so the host of the gathering is informed when the breakout room time is up. This is a useful alarm assuming that you move back from your meeting.
- Countdown subsequent to containing breakout rooms: If you check this choice, members are shown a commencement of the leftover time until the breakout rooms will end and they are gotten back to the primary session.

When overseeing breakout rooms, a significant hint is to pre-allocate clients to explicit rooms when planning the gathering. Then again, set things up so clients are relegated consequently. Understand that clients inside a lunchroom have full sound, video, and screen sharing capabilities.

Distraction Management

Zoom highlights in-meeting visit and private informing for meeting members. These can both be flipped here and there to forestall interruptions and guarantee nobody receives undesirable messages during a meeting.

Another choice you'll need to be acquainted with as a host is the capacity to switch off record move. While in-meeting moves can be useful by permitting users

to share records by means of in-meeting talk, flipping it off keeps clients from being assaulted with GIFs, images, and spontaneous content.

Disable comment, which permits participants to doodle and increase content during screen share, when expected to keep individuals from composing all around the screen.

Conclusion:

Zoom's turned into an innovator in video interchanges on the grounds that their apparatus is not difficult to utilize, and that is a significant accomplishment thinking about the number of cutting edge highlights are incorporated into their administration. Zoom keeps on appreciating unimaginable development and its item genuinely drives the way forward for the business. While Zoom doesn't offer the incorporated internet based work area arrangements of Google and Microsoft, it's unrivaled execution for video conferencing makes it an unquestionable requirement have for some experts. Then, we should investigate Facebook's new video conferencing features.

8

FACEBOO K

Feature:	Details:

Date Started	Launched in 2004. Started Messenger in 2011.
Price	Free product, supported by Advertisements.
Meeting Participants	Maximum of 50
Estimated Monthly Users	2.3 billion total users base. 1.3 billion Messenger users.
Screen Sharing	Yes
Instant Messaging	Yes, the service includes file sharing, games, and ability to send money
Unique Feature #1	The largest world user base
Unique Feature #2	Integrated into the world's largest social media network

You could contend Facebook is the single biggest stage utilized for online interchanges. Facebook initially began as a long range informal communication instrument for gatherings of understudies and has since transformed into a comprehensive web-based universe. Facebook offers three principle arrangements pertinent to online interchanges: the web-based media stage itself, the Facebook Workplace, and Facebook messenger.

Facebook's web-based media stage has turned into a peculiarity that has molded the manner in which our reality comprehends online correspondences. Facebook has over 2.5 billion dynamic month to month clients interfacing with companions, relatives, and business contacts all through the world on their foundation. Facebook upholds sharing advanced substance in pretty much every manner traversing video, picture, emoticon, message, live web based, and then some. Facebook's foundation is adapted through its high level publicizing arrangements that detailed income of $16.6 billion in 2019.

Facebook's Messenger administration has been normally incorporated into its web-based media stage permitting clients to rapidly text different clients they are companions with. Bunch discussions can be utilized for little groups to impart and video calling is accessible also. In April of 2020, Facebook declared another component for Messenger called Rooms. Rooms is an element that gives video conferencing encounters to bunches up to 50 guests. Facebook's video conferencing arrangements likewise give basic screen sharing, sound/video controls, and meeting design formats.

Until April of 2020, Facebook's primary concentration in the video interchanges space has been single direction live streaming. Later a 2016 send off, Facebook's strength in the live substance conveyance market has been equaled exclusively by Google's YouTube and Amazon's Twitch stage. Facebook developed several innovative features for live and on-demand video such as watch parties and interactive live audience polling. In 2017, the organization's organizer Mark Zuckerberg considered video a "super pattern" which would be comparable to the transition to portable. Zuckerberg has additionally said Facebook would turn into a "video first" organization in numerous ensuing interviews.

For some time in the middle 2016 and 2020, Facebook was considered to be a walled garden when it came to video content in contrast with top contender YouTube. While YouTube has turned into the best internet searcher for video content, Facebook has turned into the best web-based media framework for video.
YouTube is the world's second-biggest hunt engine.

In April of 2020, Facebook declared individuals would not need to be signed into the stage to observe live and on-request recordings facilitated on the stage. This move brings Facebook's video content to watchers without a hindrance to section like YouTube. Facebook additionally reported that it would permit makers to charge watchers for admittance to restrictive live streams.

Facebook's strength in the web-based media space has permitted the organization to spread into different spaces of online correspondence effectively on the grounds that the assistance behaves like an integral for online movement. Facebook is the world's fourth biggest site and in 2019 the normal clients went through just about one hour regularly on the stage. The lines among purchaser and business use on Facebook are moreover becoming less important.

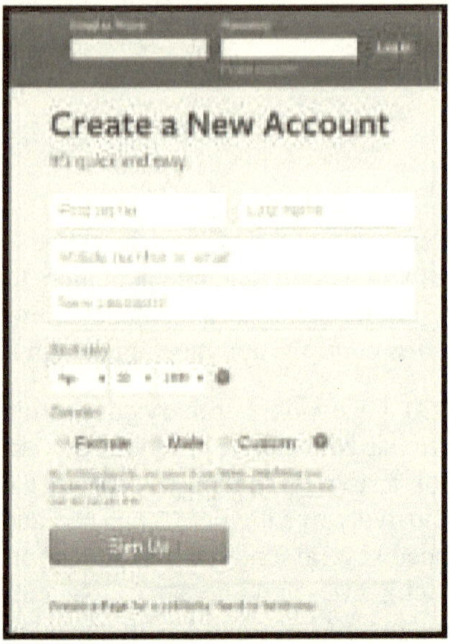

A client might utilize Facebook to remain associated with loved ones one second, and afterward utilize a similar help to interface with colleagues over a text or video call. Facebook's huge client base makes the devices more viable for correspondences in light of the fact that such countless individuals are now associated. Facebook additionally profits by a commonality clients have with the stage, permitting clients to explore different avenues regarding new administrations effectively (Metev, 2019).

While Facebook stays an exceptionally alluring answer for some, it confronted extraordinary negative public consideration from 2017 to 2019 because of protection concerns. The organization wound up paying a record $5 billion in expenses to settle protection worries with the FTC (Federal Trade Commission). The charges refered to that Facebook had inappropriately gotten private data from more than 87 million clients. Since a portion of this information was utilized by promoters during the 2016 United States Presidential political race, the negative press has been assessed to cost Facebook $37 billion (Fortune, Kelleher).

Facebook's Workplace item use a significant part of the innovation they've created for public use to give organizations a business choice and full administrator

level controls. The most effective way to ponder Facebook Workplace is a Facebook experience where the main clients on the stage are representatives of a solitary association. The whole Facebook newsfeed is utilized for organization refreshes, with remarks, gatherings, live transfers, texting, and video calling.

While Facebook Workplace doesn't offer similar kind of usefulness applications as the G Suite and Office365 it really does offer a convincing cooperation space that over 2.5 billion individuals definitely know how to use.

So where is Facebook headed? Some would say global control of online correspondences. We should investigate the Facebook Messenger instrument to more readily see how the private and gathering specialized device chips away at the stage. Since Messenger is within Facebook, you should begin by making a record or signing in with a current account.

Create an account directly on Facebook.com by filling out the short form. Once you have created an account and gained access to Facebook, connect with other contacts that you wish to communicate with. To find friends you can use the search bar at the top of Facebook. Type in a friend's name and click the search button . To send someone a friend request, click on their picture to view their profile page. On most profile pages users see an **Add Friend** button at the top of their profile page. The Add Friend button can also display inside of search results. Add Friend may not display on all user accounts depending on individual user privacy settings. Next to the **Add Friend** button are three dots that let you send a message directly or send money. Connecting with someone via Messenger doesn't require being friends on Facebook.

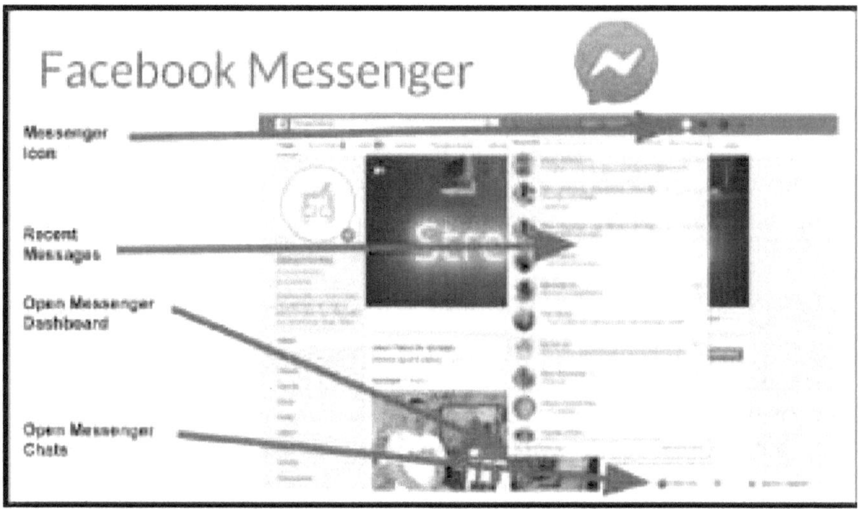

Messenger is nested at the top of the main Facebook application. By clicking the **Messenger Icon** users can easily start new messages with their connected friends and with groups of up to 250 members. Messenger can also be used to host video and audio calls for up to 50 members. Click the **New Group** in the dropdown menu or by clicking the compose buttons from the messenger dashboard to create one.

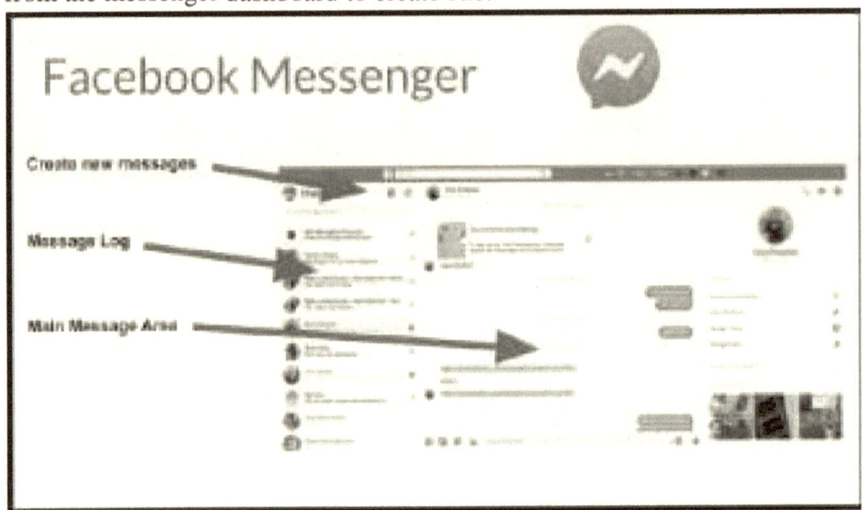

The Messenger dashboard is accessed at "https://www.facebook.com/messages" or by clicking See all in Messengers on the Messenger dropdown menu. The Messenger dashboard records each of your new discussions on the left side board. The middle board is utilized to show the chose discussion. Courier can be utilized to speak with others straightforwardly or in bunches with an assortment of media types. The most well-known type of informing is instant messages sent by essentially composing into the message region and squeezing enter.

Messenger additionally offers surveys, pictures, games, sending cash, voice messages, gifs, stickers, and documents. Surveys are an incredible component for becoming familiar with how gatherings of individuals feel about a particular inquiry. Games are a casual method for playing with companions from around the world. Facebook incorporates Words with Friends, Quiz Planet, Solitaire, and then some. Voice messages are one more incredible method for sharing media within a private message bunch. Assuming that you're acquainted with the Facebook newsfeed, Messenger incorporates practically each of similar choices for sharing media.

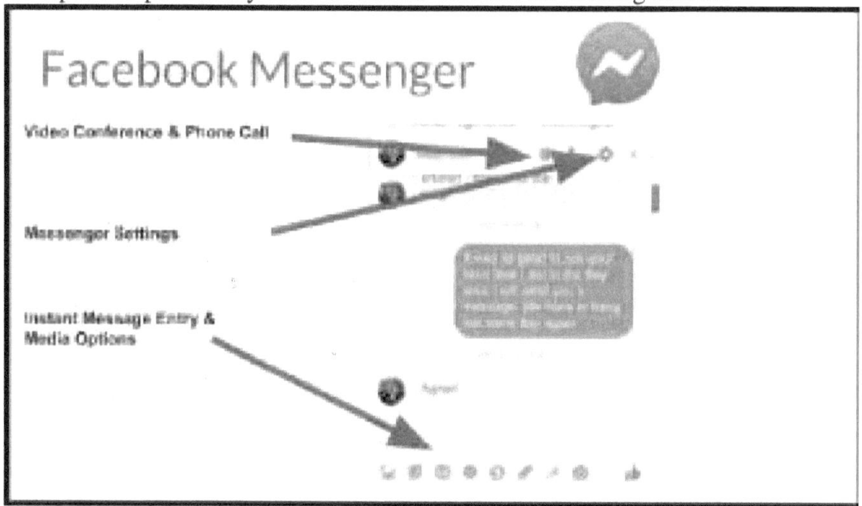

Messenger is worked off of Facebook's companion association framework, yet you can likewise message somebody without turning into their companion. Messages shipped off clients who are not as of now companions appear in a space called "Message Requests." By reacting to a message demand you're permitting that individual to speak with you, see your status, and know when you have understood messages. You can likewise click a connection in the visit box to empower I would rather not hear from to and for all time block somebody from informing you.

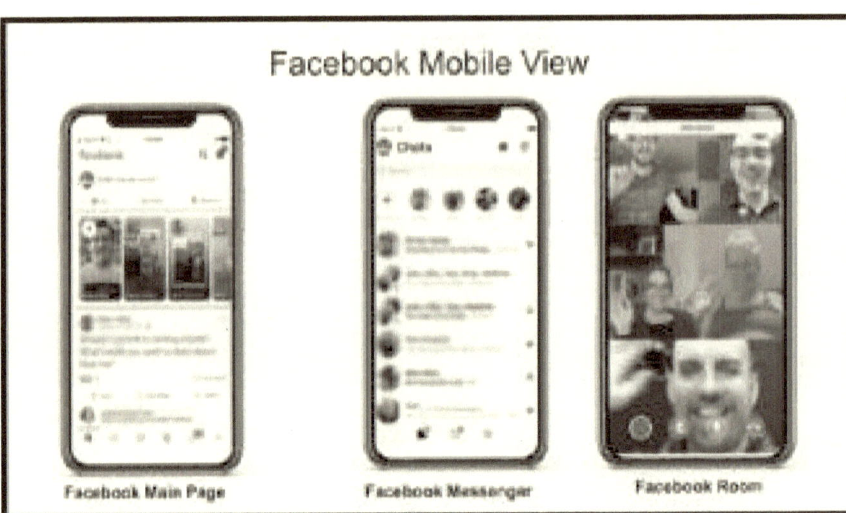

Over one billion dynamic clients of Facebook use it on cell phones. Facebook situated admittance to the Messenger stage in the upper right corner of its principle versatile application. In an internet browser, Messenger is gotten to straightforwardly through Facebook. On a cell phone, admittance to Messenger is conveyed in a different application so clients can switch between the primary Facebook experience and a committed, direct interchanges insight. Having two committed applications enables versatile clients to go straightforwardly to Messenger without opening the fundamental Facebook app.

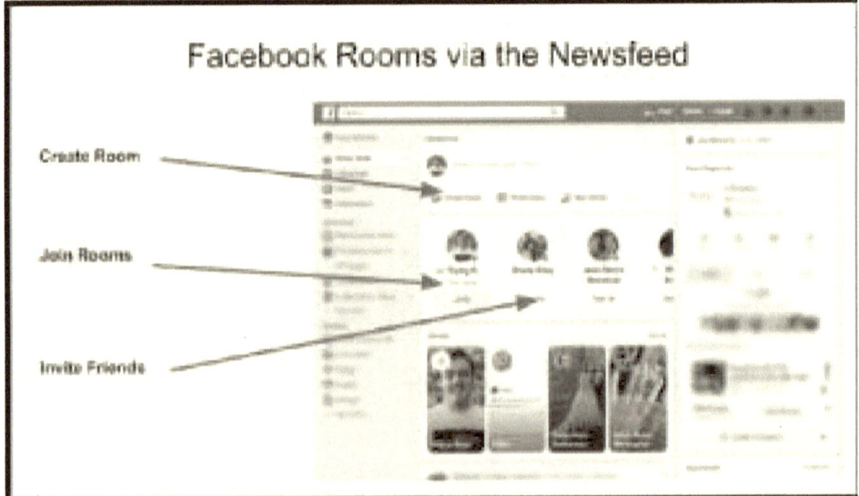

Facebook's most recent video correspondence include is called Rooms. Rooms are basically bunch video and sound visit regions where up to 50 associated companions impart. As of the distribution of this book, Rooms are being carried out as an element for Facebook clients. Facebook has declared that you can "Make a room right from Messenger or Facebook, and welcome anybody to join the video call, regardless of whether they have a Facebook account. Rooms will before long hold up to 50 individuals with no time limit." Facebook has likewise declared usefulness to "Start and offer rooms on Facebook through News Feed, Groups and Events, so it's simple for individuals to come around. "

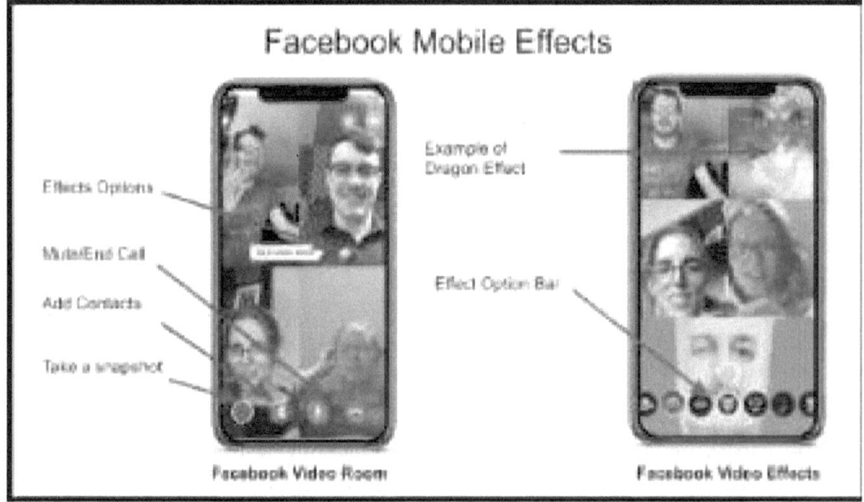

Facebook Rooms has the chance to totally change the manner in which video correspondences occur all over the planet. Facebook Rooms include the necessities for online meetings such as screen sharing, muting, chat, and two-way communications, but the features that set Rooms apart are designed for consumers.

For instance, when joining a room from a cell phone client are provoked to Tap to investigate impacts. While these impacts would be unseemly for a conference, they are exceptionally captivating for loved ones in a relaxed environment. Impacts range from increased reality channels to intuitive scaled down games. An illustration of this is the b-ball small scale game that joins a b-ball band to your face and drops b-balls from the highest point of the client's screen. Clients can move their heads to find falling balls and the game monitors the score.

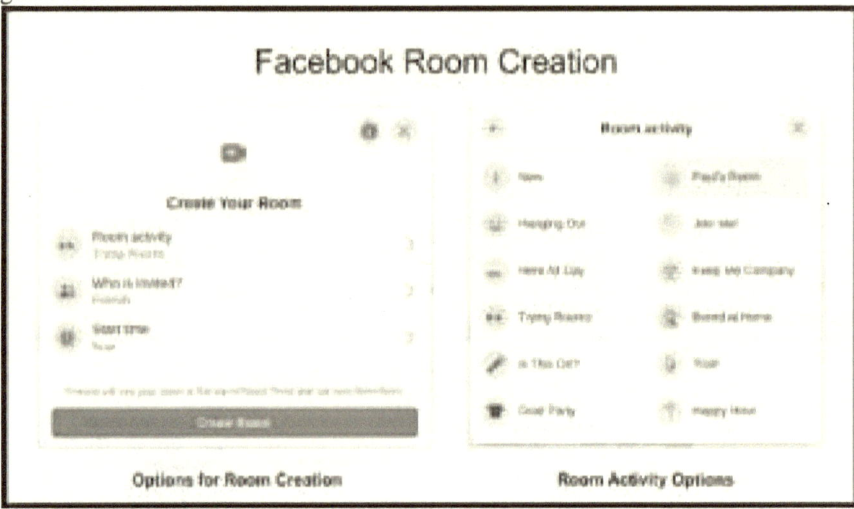

A brief glance at Facebook's recommended "Room Activity" choices shows a portion of the famous use cases which incorporate hanging out, graduate party, stay with me, exhausted at home, and party time. When you make a Facebook room, Facebook gives you a connection you can share to welcome your friends.

Facebook can likewise mechanize the gathering greeting process permitting you to just welcome all of your Facebook companions or pick explicit friends.

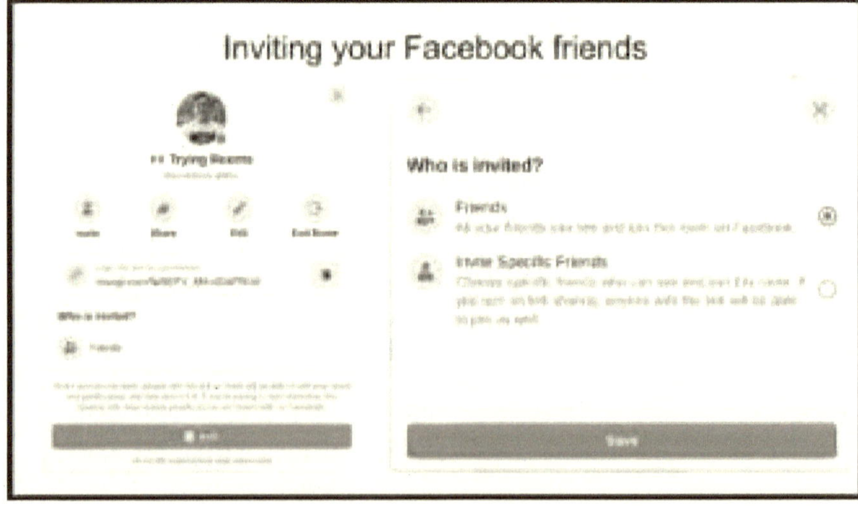

Facebook Rooms Settings & Privacy

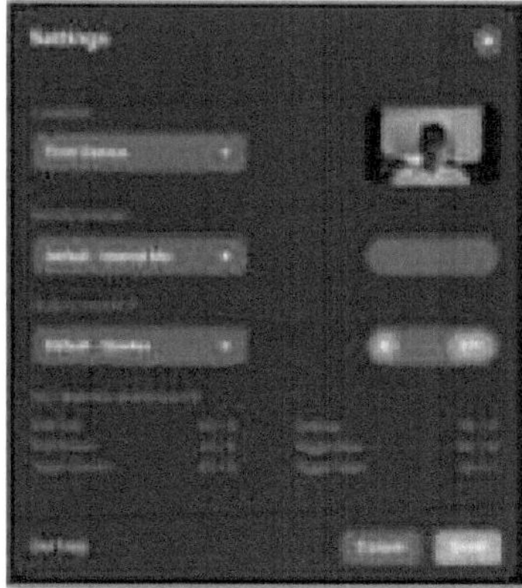

From a specialized stance, Facebook has planned probably the least demanding method for directing up close and personal video conferencing. The settings region is streamlined into three choices: select a camera, a receiver, and a sound result. Close to these choices you rapidly screen your amplifier levels and decide to play an example brief snippet to test your speakers. At the hour of send off, there are six straightforward console easy routes. Utilizing the Alt key and a letter key to rapidly end a call, enter full-screen mode, share your screen, open the settings, switch mode, and flip video.

From a security angle, Facebook has planned this instrument with three straightforward safety efforts. In the first place, Facebook is exceptionally clear with regards to who is in effect naturally welcome to your Room. Welcome your companions as a whole or pick explicit people. Past these greeting choices, the main way individuals can look into your Room is through a safe connection that you decide to share. Facebook Rooms additionally incorporates a lock room include, to impede any approaching individuals from joining. At long last, you can likewise obstruct individuals from going into your room in the future.

In 2016, Facebook put a "Go Live" button under the control of billions, totally changing the live streaming and communicated industry. In 2020, Facebook delivered a video conferencing arrangement that is novel in the

manner it mixes web-based media with online video calling. By permitting clients to share video conferencing spaces within web-based media channels, Facebook robotized the greeting system most other video correspondence arrangements required.
Similarly, Facebook Rooms can be begun in a newsfeed to naturally open solicitations to companions in a client's organization. Rooms can be begun openly gatherings or occasions to spread solicitations even further.

While Messenger stays valuable for private informing and video calls, Facebook's social sharing capacity is the explanation Rooms is ready to reform video correspondences. There are not many organizations on the planet with the client base or stage to interface companions, families, friends, and associations the manner in which Facebook can. While Facebook Rooms might appear to be a customer device, there are various business use cases for it also. Search for updates to this book as Facebook discharges improvements and new highlights to Rooms.

In the following area, you will figure out how to turn out to be more useful in online meetings.

PART 3 - Productivity Primer

Chapter 9 - Collaboration, is there a downside?

Not all cooperation is useful. In the present business climate, successful correspondence and joint effort are esteemed as key drivers of development. By and large, in a five-day week's worth of work, representatives spend between one to over two average business days going to gatherings. As per a new report, workers go through right around 31 hours every month in useless gatherings (HubSpot, 2014). Given these suppositions, most gatherings have a 40 percent shot at being ineffective. It's significant that an inefficient gathering doesn't imply that the gathering was a finished disappointment. It simply implies that most gathering participants might have been accomplishing something more useful with their time.

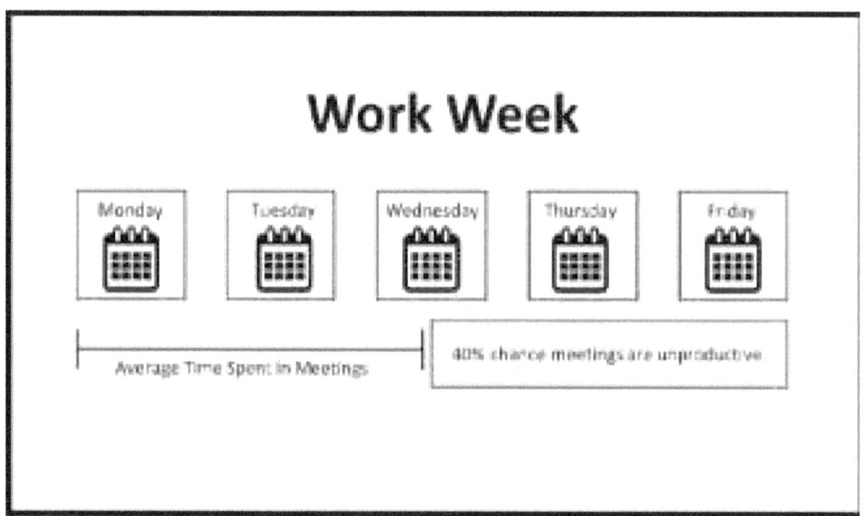

So, how might you keep representatives from going through hours in useless gatherings? Without a doubt, the vast majority of these gatherings ought to never have been planned for the primary spot. It's reasonable de rigueur for groups to work together every step of the way. Regularly, people acknowledge solely after the reality, that they've burned through significant time in useless gatherings with no plan, things to do, or settled upon expectations. A strong plan is one key to diminishing the number of ineffective gatherings workers are involved with.

Morten Hanser, the creator of Collaboration: How Leaders Avoid the Traps, Build Common Ground, and Reap Big Results, advances what he calls "restrained coordinated effort" and portrays four kinds of obstructions to collaboration.

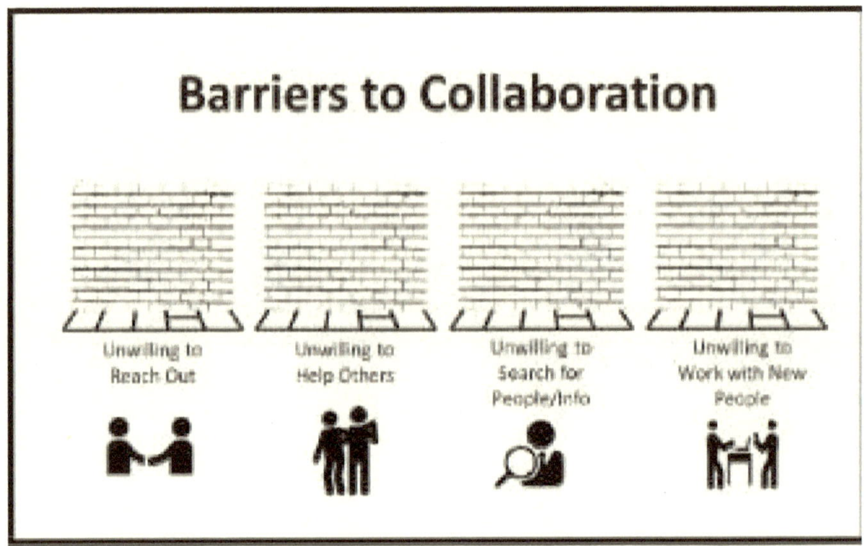

First, Hanser recognizes the "not imagined here" hindrance which depicts individuals who are reluctant to contact others. Second, the "accumulating boundary" is the place where individuals are basically reluctant to help other people. Third, is the thing that's known as the "looking through hindrance" in which individuals can't observe the specialists or data they are looking for. At long last, the "move obstruction" is the place where individuals are reluctant to work with those they don't know.

Good chiefs ought to do research to decide when the boundaries to powerful coordinated effort are excessively high for the fruitful consummation of a venture. At the point when chiefs recommend that little gatherings of informed authorities work together, they ought to consider the three stages of trained cooperation Hanser expounds on in Collaboration.

The three steps are:

1. Evaluate openings for collaboration
2. Spot obstructions to collaboration
3. Tailor coordinated effort solutions

Good administrators assist their groups with recognizing openings for coordinated effort. Managers need to mentor their teams to help them gain a working knowledge of how to effectively use available collaboration tools to tailor custom collaboration solutions which current employee workflows and whether they can be optimized.

While there are numerous coordinated effort suites and devices accessible today, none accompany a custom execution plan that is customized to your particular business needs. Hanser properly brings up that “the arrangement isn’t to get individuals to team up additional, yet to get the perfect individuals to work together on the right activities.” This is a cycle that requires direction and the board to zero in on the advancement of a particular gathering inside the company.

Most interior coordinated efforts can profit from the executives matchmaking. Administrators spot openings for joint effort, recognize hindrances and work with presentations by utilizing proper correspondence channels, like Slack, Teams, or other inside stages. The coordinate making process functions admirably for enormous organizations with directors who have P&L obligation and are incented for joint efforts that convey noteworthy outcomes. Be careful, setting up such a large number of joint effort channels can become overpowering and counterproductive. In an impending section, you’ll figure out how to enhance interchanges diverts and head off potential issues.

Businesses can profit from coordinated effort with outer accomplices also. Outside business organizations are a viable device for business advancement, however they are for the most part more hard to build up than inner joint effort projects. Some business-to-business (B2B) organizations are gainful. For instance, one business represents considerable authority in programming and the other works in equipment. Assuming that the two organizations perceive their endeavors are reciprocal, a commonly gainful association can be formed.

When looking for a B2B association, it’s vital to begin by developing an individual relationship with a contact inside the imminent business you wish to work with. These contacts are normally found on the business advancement or promoting groups of the organizations with which you wish to partner.
LinkedIn and other expert organizations are important assets for interfacing with potential business improvement and showcasing contacts. At the point when you pick possible organizations to cooperate with, research the organization’s fundamental beliefs and ensure they line up with your association’s esteems and mission. Search for ways that you can help each other for a commonly valuable relationship.

Whenever two organizations choose to accomplice, it's vital to obviously characterize jobs and obligations. During the beginning phases of exchanges, it's alright to keep things casual, as you progress, search for freedoms to all the more likely characterize the obligations on the two sides of the association. Then, draw up an agreement that clarifies roles and responsibilities in writing. In the present rapidly changing worldwide business world, outside business associations and partnerships have become quite possibly the main tool to keep a cutthroat edge.

It's not difficult to exaggerate the advantages of coordinated effort. Supervisors ought to possibly support cooperation when there's a high likelihood of useful worth. Do give groups the opportunity to deal with the devices and channels that best suit their necessities sensibly speaking. Chiefs likewise need to keep an eye out for the dangers of "over-joint effort" where groups misjudge the chance expenses of cooperation. A chance expense is basically the deficiency of potential acquires that you may have gotten from elective activities. All things considered, online joint effort is a necessary evil, and that end is expanded productivity.

Promoting trained cooperation can assist pioneers with deciding if projects that are weighty on coordinated effort are successful for their association. This vision will assist pioneers with distinguishing possible hindrances to group joint effort and assist them with proposing answers for eliminate those barriers.

Chapter 10: Four Strategies for Hosting Productive Online Meetings

#1: Are you prepared for the meeting?

The principal system for facilitating useful web-based gatherings is just arrangement. Being arranged is maybe the most remarkable methodology for facilitating useful gatherings. Arrangement empowers you to come to the gathering positive about your capacity to speak with the web based gathering apparatuses accessible. As a gathering host, you can show all participants that you're available and focusing basically by turning on your camcorder. The idea of "presence" is utilized all through web-based interchanges to unite remote groups. Many individuals feel awkward on camera yet beating this dread as a pioneer permits you to lead by example.

Why is the utilization of video so vital to facilitating useful web-based gatherings? 93% of correspondence is non-verbal, so normally advancing the utilization of camcorders during your gatherings will build your correspondence viability and member commitment. As a compelling gathering host, you should be aware of member worries about web based gathering technology.

Confronting and conquering any feelings of dread you might have utilizing on the web specialized devices is by and large the initial step you can take toward facilitating a useful internet meeting. As culture shifts, meeting on the web will turn out to be more ordinary and normal for regular correspondences. In a post-COVID world, online gatherings have turned into the standard, supplanting face to face gatherings by necessity.

Meanwhile, gatherings with loved ones online is an extraordinary method for aiding increment your solace level with innovation. Figuring out how to conquer any assumptions of uneasiness is difficult for individuals who have never chipped away at a dispersed group. The initial move toward facilitating a useful internet meeting is loosening things up and ensuring everybody in the gathering is agreeable and prepared to continue in a significant discussion.

Test gatherings are one more extraordinary way for chiefs to urge workers to acquire commonality and solace with web based gathering stages. Fun video foundations and "Final detail my appearance" highlights assist clients with turning out to be more alright with their on-camera appearance. A straightforward way to look more expert is to record a fast video on your favored gathering stage and watch it to short make changes on a case by case basis. Lighting, redid foundations, and a cleaned up setting can assist with supporting your solace level.

#2: Create consistency around meetings

As with any meeting, online meetings are more productive if you stick to a consistent schedule. Creating a consistent meeting schedule is a second strategy for hosting more productive meetings. As regularly scheduled meetings evolve, each member of the team can adapt and find their unique role within the meeting. It's important for meeting hosts to arrive at the meeting ahead of time. Think of an online meeting like a gathering of friends at a restaurant. If you arranged the gathering or made the reservation, it's always a good idea to arrive early, ensure a table is ready, and check-in with friends who have arrived early as well. Use the pre-meeting time as a chance to speak with other early arrivals. Teams thrive when professionalism and punctuality are respected at the start.

If you're booking a gathering with another gathering of individuals, put forth a valiant effort to establish an uplifting vibe for bunch cooperation. Beginning a high note will assist with guaranteeing the efficiency of future gatherings. Individuals look to a gathering host to assume liability for pushing the gathering ahead and working with information and dynamic interest. Have must conclude when the gathering should begin, following a couple of moments for relaxed discussion. Assuming that a participant rules the discussion, the gathering host might have to mediate to get the gathering in the groove again. One discrete method for pulling together the gathering is to utilize a private visit message. Another strategy is to plan progress or segue questions that can be shared during central issues in the conversation.

#3: Create and circulate a meeting agenda and notes

Meetings with a reliable timetable advantage enormously from a set up plan and meeting notes. Assuming that somebody veers off, the gathering host or co-host can allude back to the gathering plan. It's ordinary for gatherings to table or sideline discussion on an issue that goes excessively far from the planned gathering goal.

Productive gatherings have plans that are conveyed ahead of time and habitually utilize a common report for recording meeting notes. Assuming a useful discussion begins to crash the first plan, a host can make note of the data and table the discussion for survey at the following gathering. It's useful to share meeting notes in a coordinated envelope on a common drive that all gathering individuals approach. Likewise, posting the notes in a coordinated effort channel that all individuals from the gathering are a piece of is an extraordinary method for keeping projects pushing ahead.

#4: Learn to listen

Figuring out how to be a decent audience is one more key to facilitating useful gatherings. Has who do the majority of the talking need to make sure to take a respite, inhale, and tune in. A decent gathering host will pause and request input from other gathering participants. Progressing from talking mode to listening mode is likewise significant for all gathering participants. However, a review from Psychology Today observes that main 10% of individuals effectively tune in during most discussions (Osten, 2016). At times very significant is listen.

Listening to and drawing in with other gathering members consciously and insightfully is significant. Close listening additionally can empower you to publicly support groundbreaking thoughts since we gain from others' encounters. Compelling pioneers comprehend the significance of good tuning in and they appreciate it. Regardless of whether you see yourself as the "instructor" in your gathering, urge others to decipher and distil the data they've assimilated and shared it during a meeting.

Try a PechaKucha Presentation

Looking for a little motivation? Take a stab at facilitating a PechaKucha show. PechaKucha, which signifies "chatter" in Japanese, is a method of giving a story in only 400 seconds 20 pictures. Each picture gets 20 seconds during the almost seven-minute show. The thought behind PechaKucha is to introduce basic data as fast as conceivable to keep crowds occupied with a narrating interaction that they can undoubtedly understand.

The PechaKucha show design offers a reasonable start, center, and end to the story. Since each slide is allowed precisely 20 seconds, the crowd knows precisely where they are in the story. This show style offers

setting on show length for possibly restless crowds. PechaKucha forces request on narrating and gives the crowd a timetable to reference.

While PechaKucha may not be the ideal decision for each gathering, it shows the force of request in a show setting. In addition, a plan can force a settled upon request that will assist gatherings with keeping focused and stay useful. In the following section, you'll find out with regards to meeting behavior and the significance of value of voice.

Chapter 11 - Video Communication Etiquette

While video conferencing makes distant correspondence more reasonable, reliable correspondence practices can assist you with capitalizing on any internet based correspondence exertion. One system for group correspondence is classified "Value of Voice," in which every individual from a gathering is urged to have an equivalent measure of time to talk. Barry Moline, the creator of Connect, says the key to strong associations boils down to four essential interchanges strategies.

#1: Share personal stories

Sharing individual stories assists individual with joining individuals better comprehend their companions. Individual stories encourage the relationship-building process which is central to group correspondence. Put in almost no time toward the start of each gathering to assist with joining individuals assemble connections by sharing individual stories. Likewise, mesh individual stories and accounts into central issues in the gathering where accommodating; they can regularly assist with supporting key messages and develop retention.

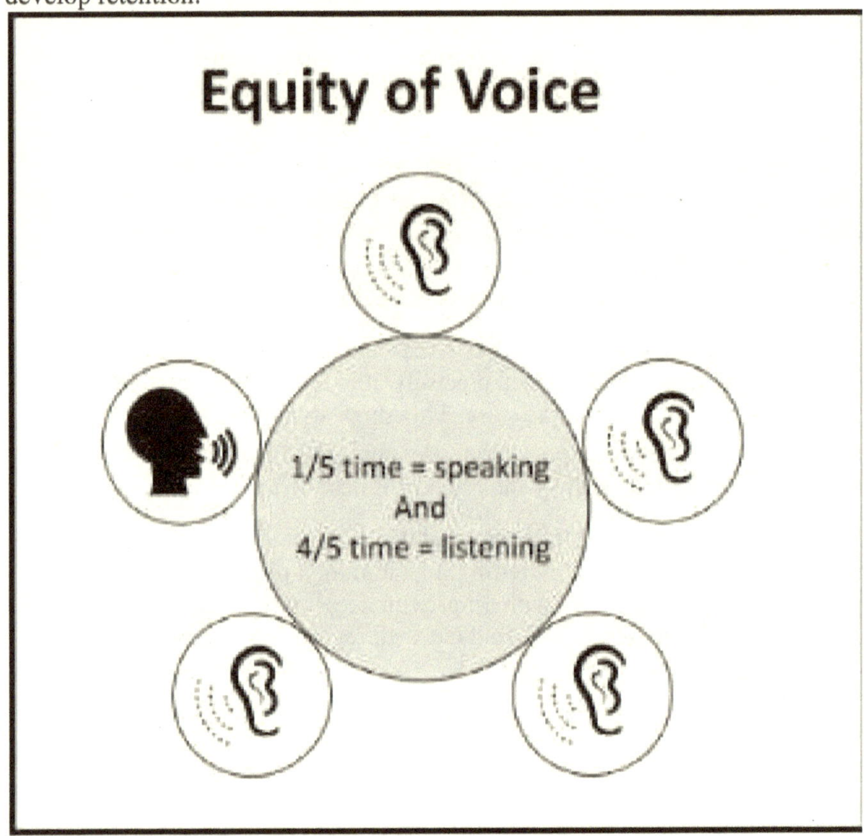

#2: Equity of voice

Achieving value of voice requires a cognizant work to offer each gathering part an equivalent chance to talk during the gathering. For instance, in a five-man meeting, every individual from the group would talk one-fifth of the time and listen four-fifths of the time. The listening side of the value of voice is the thing that makes it effective.

#3: Assume positive intent

To assist with guaranteeing useful gatherings, figure out how to expect

positive goal from
others. This suspicion helps put the gathering in a good position by zeroing in on what you really have command over - - yourself. Over and over again, the "not created here" obstruction and the "move boundary" keep meeting participants from useful joint effort. Stay away from these obstructions by empowering the suspicion of positive goal which assembles an extension for correspondence that probably won't come naturally.

#4: Value persistence

Anything advantageous sets aside time, commitment, and steadiness. When administrators distinguish joint effort projects with critical worth to the association, they need to watch out for group progress and finish. Some colleagues might lose center, avoid significant gatherings, or come to gatherings ill-equipped. Administrators can help by recognizing individuals who can fill in as joint effort project pioneers. In an impending part, administrators will figure out how to utilize social assistance to build usefulness and responsibility to assist employees with viably teaming up on projects.

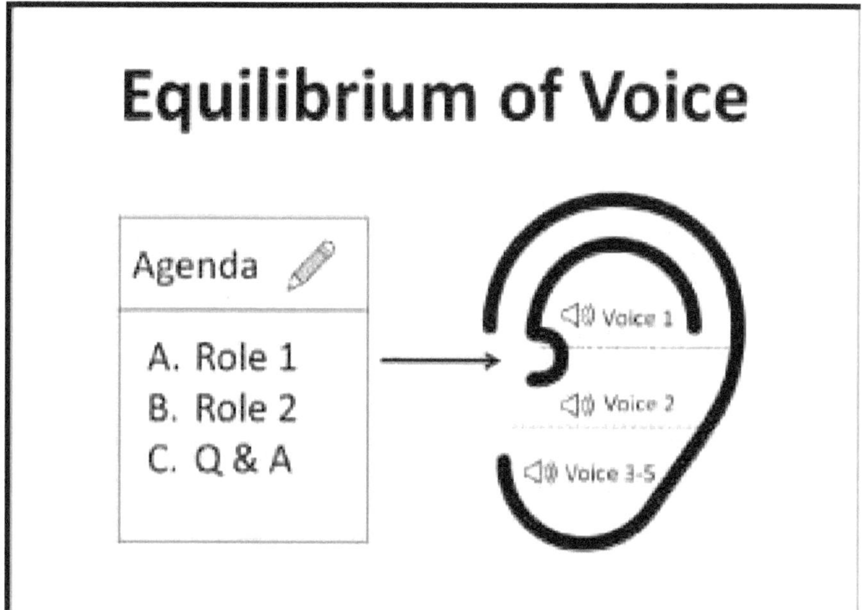

Equilibrium of Voice

Meeting pioneers might accept a novel thought I call "Harmony of Voice" to push cooperation projects a positive way. Balance of voice is a correspondence system that endeavors to boost meeting execution dependent on objectives set in a gathering plan. A gathering with an ideal balance of voice advances the most significant speakers of a gathering dependent on the set up plan and the members' jobs in the general gathering. It's exceptionally difficult for gatherings to accomplish harmony of voice without an unmistakable agenda.

Equity of voice can be great for group joint effort where a plan is currently being made and individual jobs presently can't seem to be characterized. During the beginning phases of joint effort projects, everybody should be heard particularly during pivotal group building works out. But once a team has established an agenda, subsequent meetings will benefit from an equilibrium of voice that offers subject matter experts additional focus based on the agreed-upon agenda.

How to get there

Teams can use the balance of voice by expecting all colleagues have positive purpose. For instance, a smart inquiry may just require a moment to ask yet investigating potential arrangements might take a particular colleague most of a gathering to manage potential answers.
Similarly, accomplish harmony of voice in an online class style show by offering educated authorities time to introduce their thoughts prior to posing inquiries. Meeting members can pose inquiries and get input through the techniques settled on the gathering plan. Meeting hosts ought to choose early how to oblige meeting member questions and criticism. Educated authorities are assets that groups depend on to stay informed with regards to subjects they don't have the opportunity to seek after on their own.
Meeting pioneers need to recall that well-informed authorities are a fundamental component of collaboration.

Create a detailed agenda

Another method for accomplishing balance of voice is to set up colleague jobs and adjust those jobs within a nitty gritty gathering plan. Meeting hosts can expand efficiency by organizing a plan that assists all gatherings with understanding the jobs of colleagues who have been welcome to the meeting.

A decent gathering host expects to accomplish balance of voice between all gathering members so everybody can acquire the most worth out of the meeting.

Employees at all degrees of involvement need to team up and gain from one another. Compelling gathering hosts will incorporate break-out meetings into the plan to assist with cultivating new degrees of value of voice between peers. The following is a rundown of meeting types that are great for value of voice versus balance of voice.

Collaboration Meeting (Equity of Voice)	**Presentation Meeting (Equilibrium of Voice)**
Team collaboration meeting	Expert webinar presentation
New project brainstorming	Weekly team update meeting
New employee onboarding	Employee performance review meeting
Inter-departmental collaboration	New product launch update
Educational round table	Thought leader fireside chat

Presentation meetings such as webinars, new product launches, and fireside chats, do not require equity of voice because most meeting participants come prepared to learn and absorb new information. Joint effort gatherings where groups are conceptualizing regularly benefit from taking the time needed to accomplish value of voice for all gathering individuals. At the center of the two procedures, drew in learning is the way to labor force advancement. In the following section, you will figure out how to upgrade meeting encounters to build instructive and diversion value.

Chapter 12 - Enhancing the Meeting Experience

Transformational encounters have been read up for a long time, particularly in the occasions business where shoppers consistently pay to go to experiential occasions. Joseph Pine, the writer of The Experience Economy, expounds on the method involved with catching regard for develop a groundbreaking. The most significant level of meeting commitment conjures a groundbreaking encounter for participants. While this might appear as though an encounter held for a few days of uplifting courses or a retreat, this part will urge you to consider gatherings smaller than expected groundbreaking opportunities.

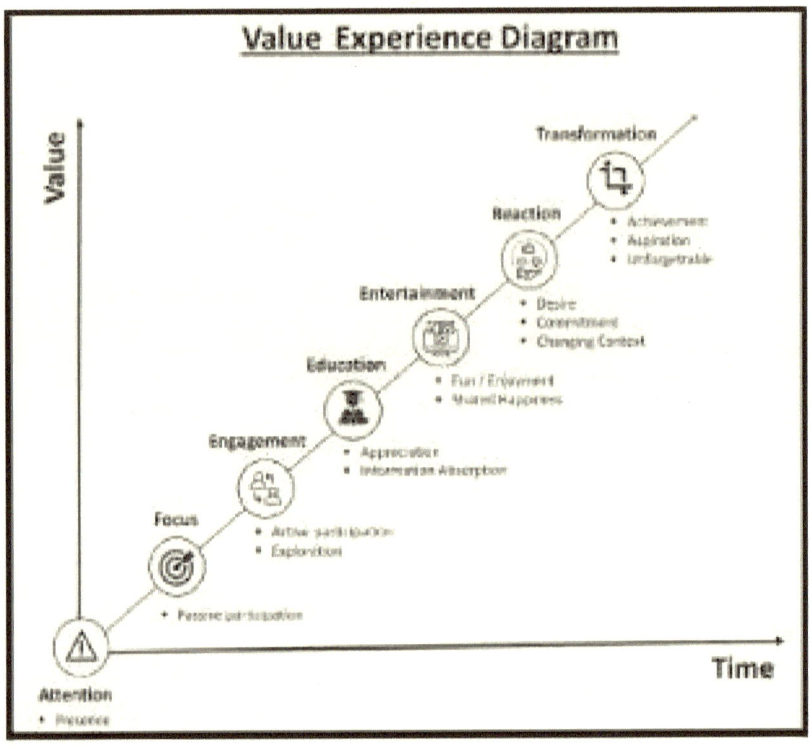

As meeting individuals hang out, consideration and center are primary to commitment. Maybe the least demanding method for conceptualizing summoning commitment in an instructive setting is another term, Edutainment. Edutainment is a course of schooling that utilizes entertainment

to draw in crowds to teach them all the while. This supernatural crossing point among training and diversion is the place where meeting members are propelled to roll out an improvement in their own lives. As gatherings progress, a decent host will empower commitment and may tailor their methodology relying upon the sort of schooling that is arranged. A decent gathering host will design out basic, however captivating focuses that have the capacity to edutain. For instance, a short test with an amusing however important inquiry can serve to "edutain" an audience.

Most gatherings will begin with detached interest which can normally develop into dynamic support as the gathering advances. For instance, aloof gathering commitment might begin with an individual scratch pad in which participants record thoughts regarding questions they might need to ask later

in the gathering. Dynamic cooperation includes posing inquiries about the content.
New coordinated effort devices can push dynamic commitment to the front line of gatherings with whiteboarding and annotation.

As the instructive interaction in a gathering normally advances, a response from meeting members can take various structures. A good response from meeting members includes a sensation of association and shared vision. Leaders can build up a feeling of shared vision by the value of voice inside a group discussion. Another good response is a sensation of motivation which could prompt an inward obligation to change for the better.

For instance, places of love might convey a Sunday administration to a huge gathering yet a short time later break out into more modest gatherings for otherworldly sharing. Within these more modest gatherings meeting participants can get to know each other better and feel more open to opening up. All changes are close to home encounters. Useful gatherings can involve customized setting to divulge positive response openings for meeting members. Assuming a change in gathering members is reached, it will probably incorporate the sensation of accomplishment and the sharing of yearnings for the future.

This could be depicted as the "AHA" second that assists you with turning a corner with the assistance of another viewpoint that was shared during the gathering. In an impending section, you'll figure out how friendly help can be utilized to share good sentiments and increment a singular's liability to act in a gathering setting.

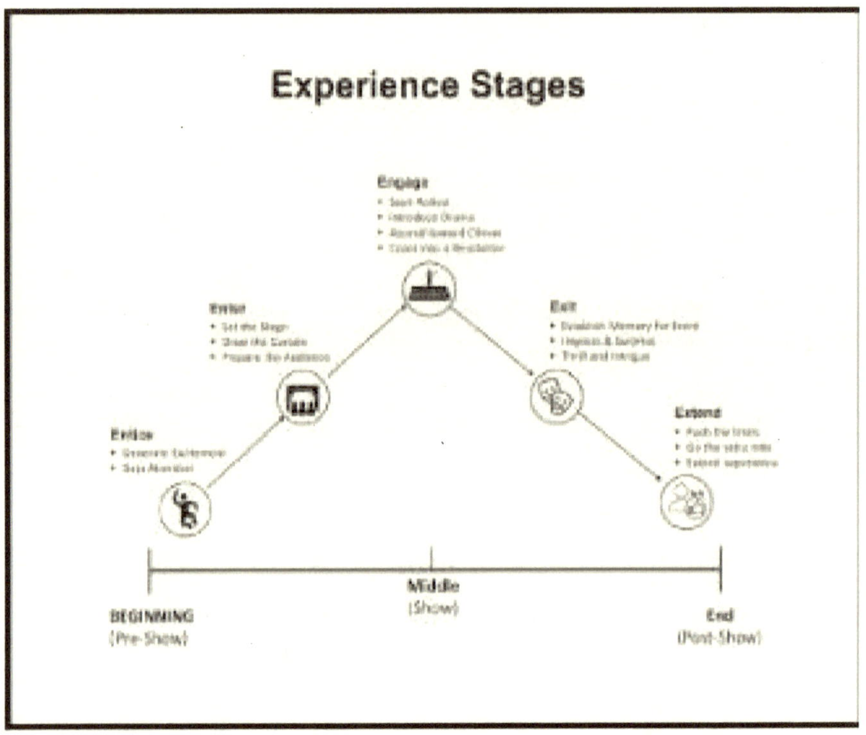

While changes are exceptionally close to home encounters, they are shareable. Assuming that gatherings happen in an open to setting and setting, individual encounters can altogether affect others when shared. Many individuals may not feel open to sharing their own encounters in huge gatherings. Consider the utilization of breakout meetings to break bigger gatherings into more modest, more personal gatherings.

Structure gatherings with a particular start, center, and end to work with the chance of change. The start of a gathering begins well before everybody gets together for a video meeting. The authority start of a gathering begins with the gathering greeting to all members. The greeting is your freedom to captivate meeting members with an intriguing plan and set the vibe for the meeting.

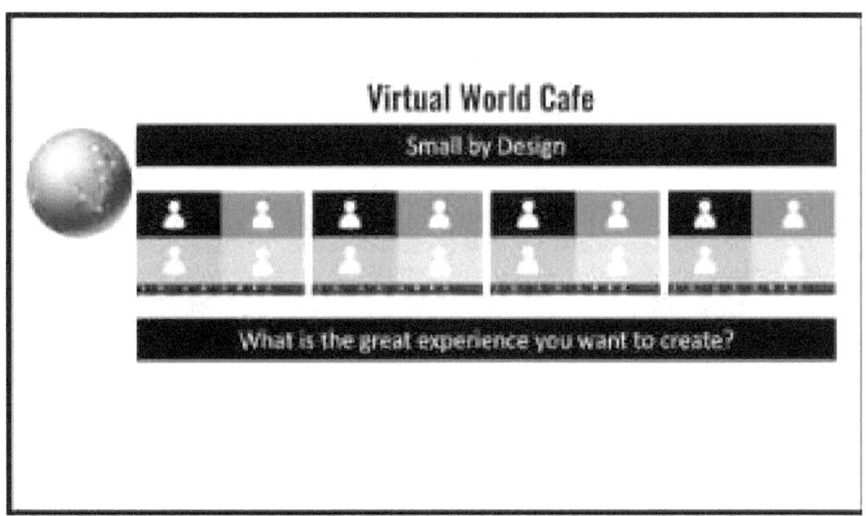

One exercise that is utilized in numerous virtual occasions is known as the "Virtual World Cafe" what separates huge gatherings into more modest gatherings of four individuals. The thought is to make them meet host who can have three individuals go along with them in a set number of rounds. The thought is somewhat similar to speed dating in groups.

Every 15 to 20 minutes three gathering participants are turned between new break out-gatherings. The host of every little gathering is liable for sharing the most influential thoughts from their past world bistro experience. Along these lines, new individuals can meet in little gatherings, and the smartest thoughts are constantly shared from past meetings.

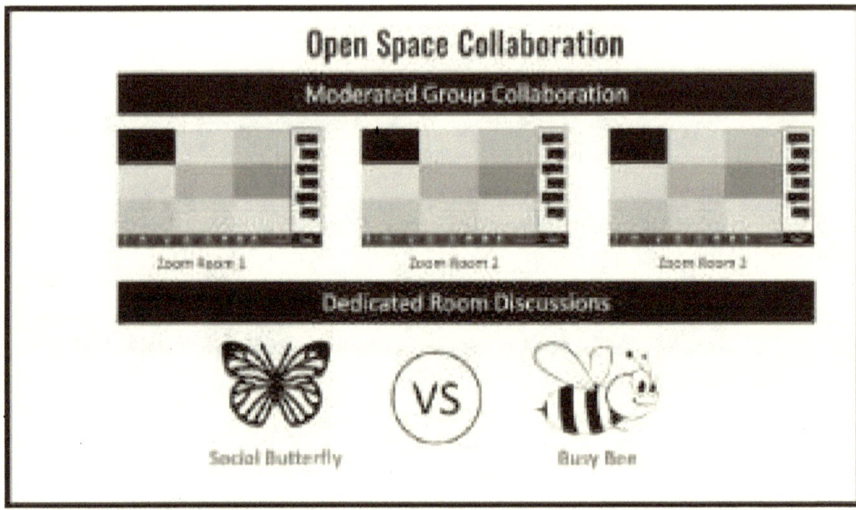

Another famous coordinated effort meeting experience is designated "Open Space Collaboration" which is an association of different autonomous gathering spaces that participants are urged to hop between. Having various discussions happening simultaneously permits members to join each gathering like an extrovert or dive into a gathering like an occupied bee.

Both cooperation meeting ideas, Virtual World Cafe and Open Space Collaboration, are demonstrated off of face to face bunch encounters. As you will definitely know, exploring a similar week by week or month to month business-related show can normally become exhausting after some time. Evaluating new imaginative ways of invigorating coordinated effort is an extraordinary method for getting gatherings to utilize the innovation gainfully. In mental examinations, this is known as the Goldilocks effect.

Gamify it

Many generally exhausting parts of a business are being rehashed to advance schooling through diversion with an interaction called gamification, a profoundly compelling method for advancing dynamic learning using a game. Gamification takes the serious components of a play and applies content into a great action. For instance, huge gatherings and meetings regularly use live random data occasions to advance dynamic learning. Live random data is an incredible way to influence a solid degree of rivalry during meetings.

Two organizations that offer web-based random data the executives frameworks are Crowdpurr and Kahoot. They can be utilized to have live democratic, tests, rivalries, and considerably more. Rivalry impacts individuals by resetting the manner in which they reference themselves against the bigger gathering. Deals rivalries, for instance, are a demonstrated apparatus for inspiring deals workers to arrive at their objectives utilizing a prize system.

While gamification and deals contests might persuade a few, Jonah Berger, the creator of Nudge, noticed that "assuming not painstakingly planned, social examinations can lead individuals to get debilitated, surrender and quit." The champ bring home all the glory model can spur individuals who get an opportunity of winning, however it can frequently abandon the remainder of the pack. Change your gamification endeavors by separating gatherings of individuals into more modest breakout meeting gatherings. Along these lines, you can direct and oversee correlation sets that representatives use to check themselves. The emphasis ought to be on solid rivalry that energizes useful commitment. Uniting explicit arrangements of individuals in little gatherings rouses individuals to work more diligently without shunning anybody for remaining at the lower part of the leaderboard. Peer strain can be an apparatus utilized for great, yet it should be managed.

Social assistance assists groups with developing responsibility for shared ventures and obligation regarding appearing and taking care of business. Berger's exploration plainly shows that companions can assist with inspiring each other to work more earnestly. The simple presence of companions can make it harder for somebody to abandon a task. Administrators can use the force of gathering presence with online correspondence to keep up with social help even with remote spread around the world.

Use a scorecard during gatherings to keep groups responsible while keeping the interaction light and fun. Custom scorecards can be made for chiefs who work with their groups on explicit ventures. Chiefs can utilize scorecards with five to ten information focuses to monitor group objectives and coordinate advancement reports that can be imparted to online cooperation platforms.

For instance, you might document your gathering notes in an organizer on Google Drive or Microsoft OneDrive. Within your gathering notes you can incorporate information from your gathering scorecards and reference recorded information for learning

purposes. Then, at that point, when you share your gathering notes utilizing a web-based coordinated effort stage like Google Chat, Discord, Microsoft

Teams, or Slack, the data is as of now coordinated and prepared for collaboration.

You can likewise smooth out cooperation by getting sorted out gathering notes and sharing data in group correspondence channels. Working together proficiently requires a forthright comprehension of who might profit from the joint efforts and who may not. Data like gathering notes and scorecards ought to be imparted to partners' administrators consider crucial for the coordinated effort process.

Once your gathering is reaching a conclusion, it's ideal to design a vital gathering exit. An all around arranged "leave technique" should uphold or support the objectives set up by your gathering plan. The finish of the gathering is an incredible opportunity to give associates approval for nicely done. Assuming you have a convincing source of inspiration that you are putting something aside for the finish of your show, consider uncovering it inside a particular bound together joint effort channel. For instance, maybe you have a blog entry that sums up your thinking on a specific subject you're meeting about. Consider posting a synopsis in a Slack channel with a connection to the whole blog entry just later your gathering. For instance: "An outline of our discoveries will be posted in the 'clear' Slack channel. Kindly go ahead and push the discussion forward there assuming you have extra contemplations over the course of the following several days."

Thinking through your leave methodology is an incredible method for closing gatherings with reason. Consider advancing ground breaking thoughts that can be utilized to sum up your gathering's motivation and support coordinated effort on need projects.

The role of small group meetings

Malcolm Gladwell developed the possibility of social assistance in his book The Tipping Point in a couple of significant ways. Gladwell concentrated on Methodism's organizer John Wesley, and his 4,000-mile venture over horseback meeting with little gatherings. Wesley made a trip from one town to another and remained in every town adequately long "to frame the most energetic of his believers into strict social orders, which thus he partitioned into more modest classes of twelve or so individuals," as per Gladwell. Every little gathering was urged to go to week after week gatherings and live by the severe Methodists

standard. Gladwell takes note of that "Wesley understood that to achieve a crucial change in individuals' convictions and practices… you expected to make a local area around them."

In the following part, you'll realize the reason why little gatherings are so powerful for interchanges and you can figure out how to put together your online correspondence channels.

Chapter 13 - Organizing Collaboration Channels

All organizations are in a consistent condition of progress. In The Grid, creator Matt Watkinson, clarifies why the customary method of concentrating on business as a static framework is inadequate. Generally Watkinson says that organizations like to "separate things into little pieces, and afterward concentrate on them in disconnection." While your association might see solid outcomes from facilitating numerous little gatherings with devoted groups, it's regularly hard so that these little gatherings could see the master plan. As a general rule, all organizations are interconnected frameworks where one choice influences different spaces of the framework. Administrators need to stay took advantage of the cooperation endeavors of their colleagues to search for all-encompassing circumstances and logical results situations that can result from little group choices. For this reason huge "all hands" update gatherings are likewise significant for interfacing offices under a typical vision.

Regardless of how enOr on the other handmous or little a gathering is, it's a significant exercise to consider the most ideal result for all gatherings when you unite individuals for a gathering. When you have a thought of the most ideal gathering results you can endeavor to take shape the thought into a show slide. Significant level show slides can prime gathering participants for the ideal gathering result. You might choose to show this sort of slide toward the start of a gathering, or toward the last snapshots of a gathering to share a source of inspiration. You can generally download a solitary slide from PowerPoint or Google Slides as a picture. Or, embed a solitary gathering result slide as a connection on schedule solicitations to share a slide that primes participants for your meeting.

As associations keep on pushing the limits of joint effort, a feeling of "computerized immersion" can mess our lives and diminish usefulness. Assuming that you've as of now lost significant thoughts within your online joint effort suite, it's an ideal opportunity to put together your group's computerized system. In the Tipping Point, Gladwell audits an idea in intellectual brain research known as "Channel Capacity" which clarifies the cutoff our cerebrums have for sorting explicit channels of data. Tests were led utilizing an assortment of situations to test the capacity of human memory to arrange and review information.

"The Magical Number Seven"

One model comes from Bell Laboratories as it chose the number of numbers to remember for a standard phone number. Chime needed to utilize in excess of seven digits yet later it tried the memory of many individuals, the organization observed that they struggled recollecting number strings past seven digits. This broadly became known as "The Magical Number Seven" and it clarifies why phone numbers are seven numbers in length. Gladwell notes: "As individuals… we can indeed deal with a limited amount a lot of data without a moment's delay. When we pass a specific limit, we become overpowered… [with] our capacity to handle crude data." (Gladwell, 2000).

Gladwell likewise calls attention to that the idea of human channel limit additionally applies to social channel limit. A British anthropologist named Robin Dunbar notes, "hundred and fifty [people] appears to address the greatest number of people with whom we can have a really friendly relationship with knowing what their identity is and how they identify with us."

Gladwell takes note of that the gathering size of 150 comes up in history over and again as the biggest number of individuals in a gathering that can be coordinated and still keep up with significant relationships.

A fascinating illustration of this comes from a strict gathering called The Hutterites that has an arrangement set up to part the size of a state when it comes to 150. Since the distribution of The Tipping Point, numerous organizations have adjusted to this model and decreased the size of their associations into more modest, more significant gatherings. Gore Associates is a company that has used this rule of 150 to manage their company, successfully dividing up divisions into groups of 150 even when their plants are right next door to each other.

Small group meetings and sympathy groups

While enormous associations of individuals can turn out to be more productive by working in more modest gatherings of 150 or less, little gathering gatherings can likewise profit from restricting gathering size. Human mental ability, which restricts our capacity to decipher crude information, is unique in relation to our passionate limit, which restricts our capacity to associate with others. Gladwell refers to something therapists call the "Compassion Group" to assist with clarifying the quantity of individuals in our lives we can genuinely mind profoundly about.

The exploration shows that by and large, individuals will list 12 individuals who they're generally associated with. A great many people are simply ready to think often profoundly about a gathering of 10 to 15 people in their lives. This is like the "Sorcery Number Seven" thought where people start to over-burden their capacity to recognize such a large number of channels of exceptional data. Every individual from a cooperation meeting is a channel of special data that others in the gathering need mental space for. Consequently, making little joint effort bunches further develops addressing efficiency.

These thoughts support the need to smooth out the way associations collaborate

by making just as numerous special cooperation channels as are essential. Chiefs need to restrict coordinated effort channels to the individuals who can genuinely profit from them. Supervisors ought to effectively look for criticism on the significance of correspondence channels to keep channels useful for the colleagues who use them.

Communications channels will continually change, and their pertinence to explicit representatives will change as your business needs develop. Permitting individual colleagues, the opportunity to quiet or nap channels of correspondence is a decent initial step for paring down channels. Supervisors ought to consistently scrutinize the requirement for new channels before they're made. An excessive number of channels can make clients befuddled with respect to where they should post discussions and work together. Pare down to just however many one of a kind channels as important to cause it clear where joint effort ought to happen.

Organizing tools

A coordinated record sharing framework is an establishment for a useful web-based work area. If conceivable, take a stab at restricting any single level of your common envelope association to something like is important. Thusly, your group can make envelopes for every coordinated effort project within an instinctively coordinated design. Groups can save records straightforwardly in coordinated envelopes and effectively review precisely where explicit documents ought to be located.

For instance, save a report and the information the report references within a similar organizer. With present day internet based work areas, you can even archive together and reference imparted organizers to hyperlinks. The incredible thing about cloud-based recording frameworks is that each record has a hyperlink that can be connected inside different reports. At the point when you share a document in a group joint effort channel, that record can likewise incorporate connections to different wellsprings of data that are coordinated in their individual common folders.

Meeting notes, for instance, can reference scorecards, deals information, or other applicable materials. At whatever point your group has an inquiry regarding the deals from an earlier month, observing the information and important reports is simple and efficient.
Once your group is prepared on the manner in which the association structures the information, looking for data turns into a straight way rather than a depleting computerized maze.

Chapter 14 - Priming for Productive Meetings

There's a cycle in brain science called "preparing" that is useful in gathering planning. Preparing is a useful asset for meeting has on the grounds that it assists with affecting the manner in which meeting members will connect their job in relationship with the proposed gathering. Research shows that preparing can influence someone to walk more slowly by having them read words such as "patient," "polite," or "respectful." So, prime your meeting participants to be excited for an upcoming meeting using words such as "impressive" or "tremendous." Depending on the kind of show you're arranging, consider preparing your gathering participants with an appealing title or a related picture appended to the gathering invitation.

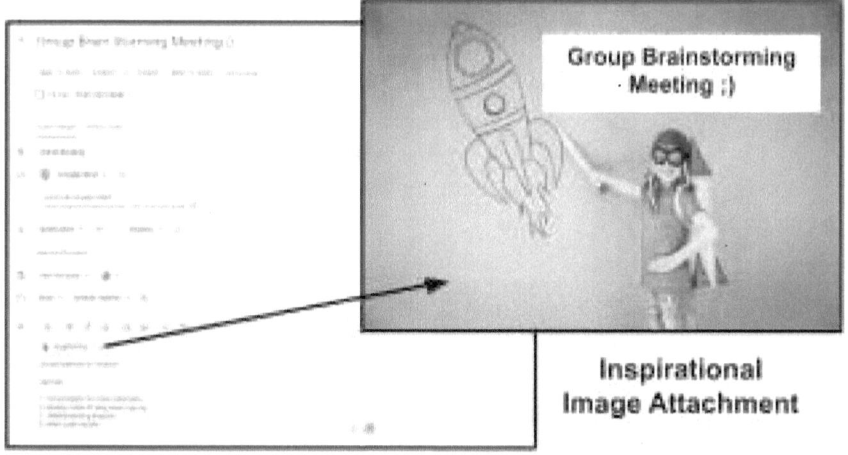

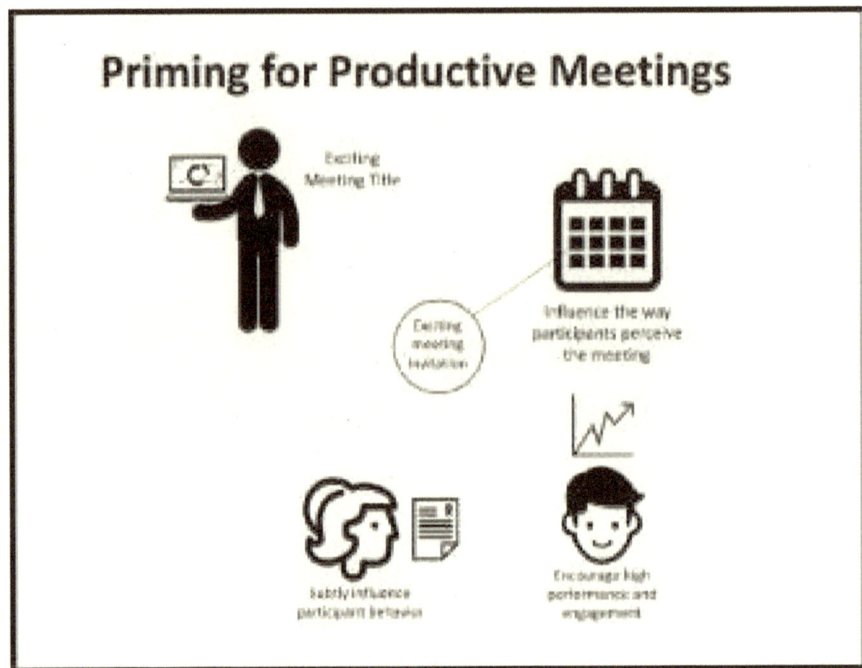

Take a second to consider the sort of preparing that would be useful for your next gathering. As a gathering host, you need to foster a standing for booking drawing in and helpful gatherings. As a gathering member, you need to take part in smart commitment that gives everybody esteem, except you additionally need to safeguard your own time from useless meetings.

The gathering plan itself is a device that can be utilized to prime participants for a positive encounter. The additional time you put into the gathering plan, the almost certain your gathering participants will come ready to lock in. You can conceptualize helpful words via looking on Google. Consider looking for "energizing words" or "connecting with words" that you can incorporate assisting better with characterizing the motivation behind your next meeting.

Set Yourself up for Meeting Success

Once you have made way for your next gathering the time has come to get the sorcery going. You have effectively pre-arranged the plan and your gathering participants know about every individual who is joining in.

Contingent upon the sort of meeting that you are facilitating, you probably will need to prepare key gathering members with extra information.

Collaboration gatherings are by and large the most straightforward to have on the grounds that the result is basically founded in a group sharing plans to accomplish a typical goal.
Presentation gatherings regularly require more coordination between key well-informed authorities and meeting participants. Gatherings that include informed authorities offering content to crowds of in excess of twenty advantage from a mindful gathering moderator.

Moderators sort out inquiries from a group of people and curate crowd commitment without disturbing the moderator's line of reasoning. A basic registration call before the gathering is frequently to the point of preparing a key gathering participant for progress. You can likewise post a survey in an important cooperation programming channel before a gathering to measure interest from different gatherings in your association. A tiny amount of exploration can make a huge difference toward directing your gathering's plan and connecting with your gathering participants' interests.

Engaging huge crowds is here and there simpler than little gathering crowds. Jonah Berger, the creator of Invisible Influence, investigates how friendly impact can influence everything from the items individuals purchase to the fulfillment they feel for their occupations. Berger's exploration takes note of that "individuals don't believe they're affected by others... however 99 point nine percent of all choices are formed by others." Large crowds can be overseen cautiously utilizing meeting control devices to decidedly affect meeting usefulness. For instance, enormous gatherings benefit from including questions voiced straightforwardly from meeting participants. However, without control, most web-based gatherings can be loaded up with individuals slicing each other off attempting to figure out who should talk straightaway. A decent mediator can handle the crowd's capacity to unmute their amplifiers utilizing the lift hand feature.

Large audiences can enjoy the benefit of shared online spaces for engagement such as chat rooms and break out collaboration areas where positivity can thrive when properly moderated. A functioning visit room, for instance, can start inventive thoughts and urge aloof participants to draw in with the activity.

Facilitate positive engagement

Meeting arbitrators cultivate positive crowd commitment while discouraging possibly regrettable consideration too. One method for cultivating positive commitment is to come to the gathering ready with a rundown of interesting inquiries. These inquiries can be gone into the visit room all through your gathering to empower commitment all through your gathering. Consider making a rundown of inquiries that lead up a climactic "defining moment" question. A defining moment question accepts your gathering participants know about the topic. Utilize a defining moment question to apply instructive topic to a genuine circumstance that applies setting to your particular business.

Turning point questions can likewise be left open-finished. Open-finished inquiries are an incredible method for exitting a gathering and leave your participants thinking. Defining moment questions that are interesting can have an especially beneficial outcome. Well known images are an extraordinary hotspot for defining moment media that can incite giggling. Images increase the value of make instructive substance more paramount. A recent report observed that 74% of individuals send images to make individuals grin or snicker and 53 percent send them to respond to something. Your organization should have a collaboration system that can be used for communication before and after important meetings. You can suggest that subsequent conversations happen in explicit channels on your correspondence stage. For instance, toward the finish of your gathering, you can say, "how about we follow this up with your thoughts in the "showcasing' channel."

The Cliffhanger Exit

One methodology that energizes efficiency later a gathering is a cliffhanger exit. What will shock us most with regards to this subject at the following week's gathering? There is no compelling reason to over-think your gathering exit. *The Invisible Influence takes note of that "simple openness [to other people] expands loving*." The more you meet with your companions, the more grounded your connections will turn into. The more drawn out term your relationship-building endeavors are, the less significant it is to set up an astounding exit.

Instead, check whether you can foster an inside joke with your group. Incredible running jokes are open-finished, and they can assemble group associations with a straightforward association point. Concentrates on show that the more individuals see something, the more they will like it and commonality prompts enjoying. In this way, basically "Showing Face" and introducing your thoughts regarding any matter ought to forever be viewed as an advantage for relationship-building. Time is cash to many individuals however maybe, more critically, time is an encounter that can be shared.

Joseph Pine, the creator of the Experience Economy, takes apart the distinction between "time very much saved" and "time all around spent" to investigate the worth of shared encounters. Time all around saved, is by and large connected with recruiting somebody to play out an assistance that requires some investment than it would the individual employing them. Time very much spent, is associated with more valuable experiences such as team building, events, and vacations that are shared with others. For instance, time all around saved could be helping somebody through a technical support issue. Time well spent, would work together on new use cases for innovation that can be applied to business and building an enduring relationship with a collaborator in the process.

A fascinating part of social impact is the capacity meeting has need to urge individuals to perform better as they rally behind a thought. Norman Triplett, the researcher credited with the introduction of social brain science, demonstrated this hypothesis by contemplating serious cycling.

Triplett's review, which turned out during the 1800s, demonstrated that cyclists cycled quicker when they dashed against a gathering of others. His peculiarity is designated "social assistance" and it clarifies why individuals perform better within the sight of others. Applying social assistance to meeting usefulness requires a comprehension of social impact. It turns out that the presence of others can have a positive or negative effect on performance depending on how complex the task is.

In the 1920s, Stanford teacher Bob Zajonc demonstrated that straightforward assignments like riding a bicycle by and large see further developed execution within the sight of others. But, more complex tasks like trigonometry performed in the presence of others will, on average, decrease performance.

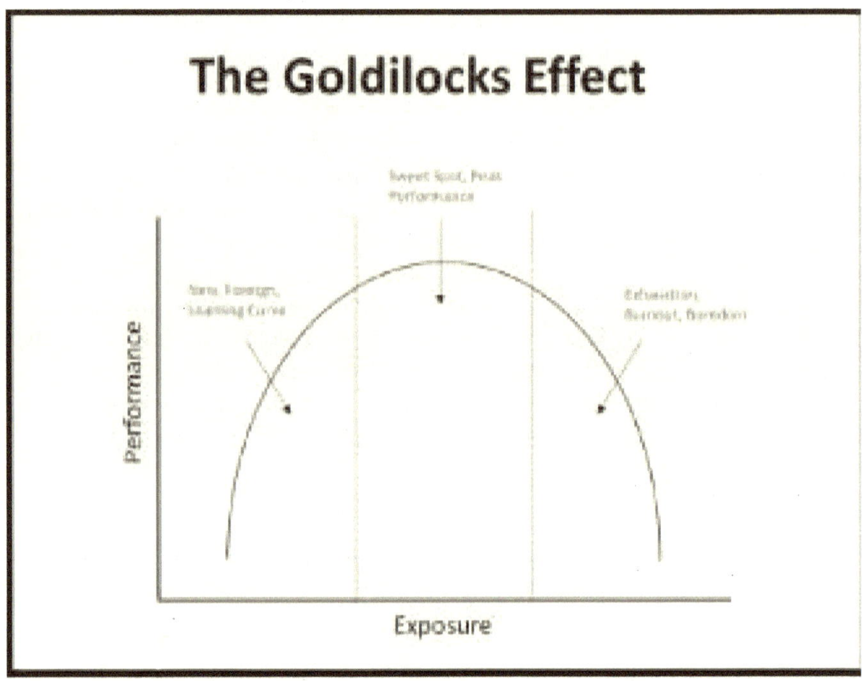

It is feasible to build your impact by basically meeting with individuals all the more every now and again. The Goldilocks impact might disclose why rehashed openness to others and thoughts can build our love for them. Rehashed openness to something can assist individuals with turning out to be more acquainted with it. In his book the Invisible Influence, Jonah Berger clarifies how the Goldilocks impact regularly follows an "upset U-shape direction." This clarifies why something new is at first unfamiliar, and along these lines individuals at first feel pessimistic toward it.
Then, later expanded openness, when things become more recognizable, individuals respond decidedly. Toward the finish of the U-molded bend, on the off chance that you have an excess of openness to a certain something, you might feel exhausted and again feel contrarily toward it. This is the ordinary Goldilocks-modified, U-molded direction of affection.

The well known "Demise by PowerPoint" saying summarizes the number of individuals feel about standard conferences. Gatherings with new thoughts are bound to draw in a group of people. In this way, it turns out to be progressively critical to keep your gathering content new, the more you keep on gathering with the same

crowd after some time, or you hazard losing the interest of your gathering participants.

Think about the early phases of the Goldilocks impact of another chief. At first, your new boss is unfamiliar to you and your experience is mediocre at best. Over the long run, your supervisor acquires your trust and turns into a pioneer you gaze upward to. It's workable for incredible pioneers to "resist the pattern" and keep on rousing others over a long and effective profession. I call this the Goldilocks Extension Process.

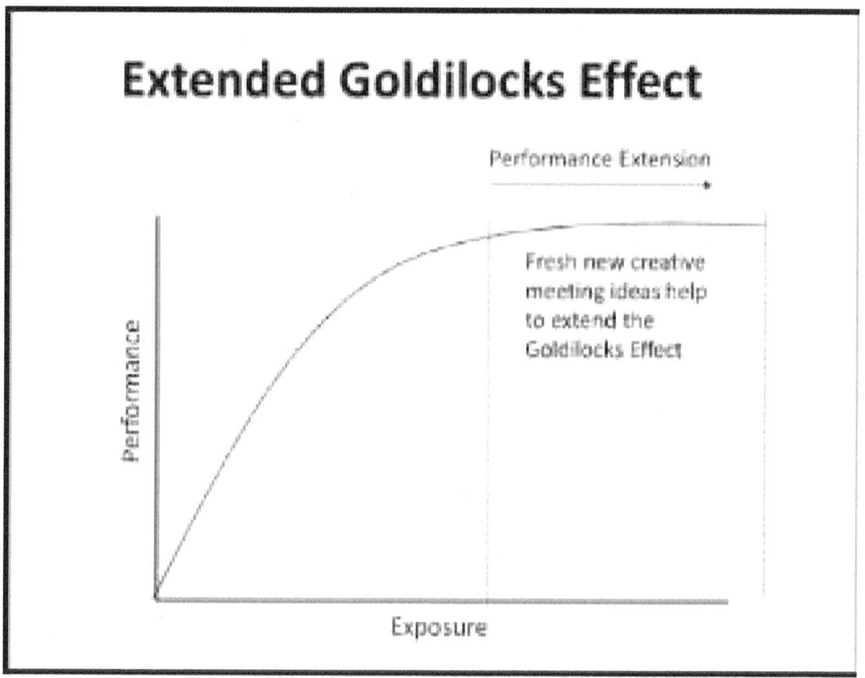

Passion and inventiveness are devices people can use to broaden the Goldilocks impact and level in a useful space. Human connections are dynamic and online interchanges enable us to effectively reestablish our connections and work together to fabricate further associations that can endure forever. At the point when groups can beat difficulties together, their connections develop further decidedly. Broadening the goldilocks level is when connections transform in vocation associations that can transform into inheritances of

teamwork.

Chapter 15: Hosting a Captivating Webinar

Eventually in your online interchanges venture, somebody in your association will need to have an online class. Online classes are online gatherings that highlight at least one specialists who make a show to an enormous group.
Before you get convinced to host or joining an online course inquire as to whether a customary gathering configuration will get the job done. Online courses require significantly less gathering participant investment than an ordinary gathering. Accordingly, more centered consideration around show quality is needed for online course has. Online courses are regularly publicized to huge crowds and they guarantee worth to the crowd as information.

Webinars by and large element a standard drawn out design that effectively squeezes into the timetables of invested individuals. It is critical to remember that individuals are occupied and will leave an online class that doesn't draw in their inclinations inside a couple of moments. Practically all online classes are recorded and made accessible for the people who enlisted yet didn't make it.

Our group at the StreamGeeks has facilitated great many online courses throughout the long term. In that time, we have produced strong instructive and engaging recordings that shape our online presence. We utilize the force of web-based media to disperse our online courses and increment viewership by multiple times. Like most organizations, we began our excursion into a video by facilitating online courses with a straightforward stage called GoToMeeting. We then moved over to Zoom, which is our platform of choice for video communications.

In our latest live transmissions, you will see that we use Zoom for correspondences with our live crowd. Before we began utilizing Zoom within our live transmissions, our group would live transfer straightforwardly to YouTube, Facebook, and LinkedIn utilizing programming called vMix. A few organizations use online class stages to create leads by gating admittance to the substance. While this might appear to be worthwhile, over the long haul, the absence of extra openness that is acquired through web-based media might end up turning into a bottleneck for online growth.

We've observed a center ground wherein you can utilize live communicating via web-based media and still deal a gated secure Zoom meeting for power clients. It's significantly more successful to offer your online courses via web-based media stages when
you will probably arrive at a greatest number of web-based watchers. In our

latest transmissions, the utilization of Zoom gatherings as a type of two-way correspondences inside a bigger single direction broadcast has improved our narrating abilities impressively. It has additionally made a cooperation space for our crowd that incorporates the significant gathering presence that makes taking in encounters come alive.

From the watcher's viewpoint, it is a lot simpler to watch an online course on YouTube than on stages that require a product download. In the wake of facilitating many online classes, the information shows that our particular crowd favors the YouTube experience. YouTube can essentially sit inside any internet browser and can even be played behind the scenes while watchers accomplish other work.
Downloading new programming for each online course that somebody needs to watch can be awkward and may cause contact among you and your viewers.

On the other hand, online class stages offer numerous significant elements that make them advantageous for significant occasions. For instance, the lift hand include effectively helps online course arbitrators observe intrigued members who need to pose inquiries. Other Q&A and surveying highlight really makes online class bundles intended for undeniable degrees of learning and crowd commitment. It's significant that while online course programming regularly requires a download, the exceptional experience is probably going to be a more comprehensive experience.

At the day's end, the main component for commitment is content. Content is continually ruler. On the off chance that you have a decent heartbeat on what your crowd reacts to, you can mine your best substance thoughts from their inquiries and transform it into subjects for future webinars.

Instead of zeroing in on forthcoming lead age, center around content and the worth you intend to convey during your online course. Indeed, think about how to teach participants, yet more significantly, ask how you will convey esteem within as far as possible set by your online course. Ponder how participants will invest their energy with you. What do you need them to detract from the experience? At last, the more you care about your crowd the better you will associate with it.

By expanding your online course's show quality, develop your crowd naturally. As you keep on making online classes with high presentation quality, the replay worth will expand, which will develop your general crowd. You'll begin to see watchers remarking on your YouTube recordings and sharing them on Facebook and different stages. An expanded spotlight on the worth of your substance gives your online courses a more extended timeframe of realistic usability. Our group has recordings that keep on connecting with online crowds' a long time later the online courses were posted on friendly media.

Depending on how you position your online course, it can turn into an incredible apparatus for practically any space of an association's correspondence plans. Online classes can draw in new possibilities, connect with existing clients, and fabricate connections in the business pipe. At the point when you center around the nature of your online course content, your interchanges objectives become a lot more straightforward to achieve.

Chapter 16: Innovations in Video Communications

Video correspondences and content conveyance advances have gone through a stunning time of development and change over the previous decade. Video conferencing innovation has moved to the cloud permitting anybody, anyplace, to interface and speak easily. Live video real time has advanced into web-based media putting a "go live" button under the control of billions of clients. This democratization of innovation has prompted a wide range of new use cases. All through this cycle organizations like Twitch, Facebook, Zoom Video Conferencing, Google, Microsoft, Slack, and Discord have all accomplished hazardous development by paying attention to clients and scaling their contributions to match developing business sector requirements.

In this part, find out with regards to advancements in live web based, video conferencing, and content conveyance. Seeing how to involve the most recent elements in live web based, video conferencing, web-based media, and joint effort programming will assist you with planning vivid encounters for online participants. To convey these product arrangements, first contemplate your occasion and its relationship to community. Will your gathering be public, private, or a blend of both?

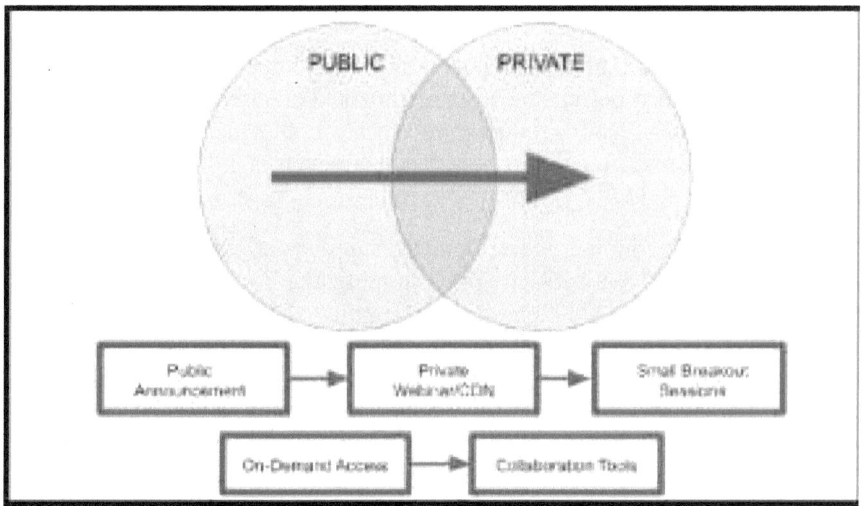

Social media sites - like Facebook Live - are ideal objections for purely public occasions since they offer the biggest measure of openness and shareability. In any case, numerous gatherings are held in a private setting where just explicit gathering participants ought to approach. Private gatherings influence video meetings and online classes that require exceptional gathering solicitations with discretionary passwords or online course enlistment. Facilitating a private online course or video gathering is a simple method for facilitating private introductions that offer client commitment apparatuses in a private setting.

For instance, you might have a Zoom meeting with a little gathering of dear companions while a Zoom online course could have a web-based occasion with up to 100 intuitive video members and up to 10,000 view-in particular. Zoom offers a cloud-based dashboard that furnishes occasion chiefs with a solitary spot to oversee enlistments and incorporations with existing CRM frameworks. The Zoom online class framework, and most others on the lookout, offer live Q&A, surveying, participants can lift their hands, and there's even a consideration sign component. For gatherings where you need to adapt access, Zoom offers a PayPal combination through an assistance called Zapier.

One of the most creative new elements reported at the 2019 Zoomtopia meeting is live interpretations. Zoom has upheld programmed video records, a component that gives discourse to message document handling in the cloud, starting around 2017. The new interpretation include gives live interpreters who can decipher your gathering progressively and convey the made an interpretation of sound to gatherings of members all over the planet. This new component permits meeting members to choose their gathering language of decision from a rundown of accessible live mediators. Meeting members will hear the mediators at 80% sound levels and the first speaker at 20 percent.

Video conferencing industry developments supplement gatherings and live streams in numerous ways. While programming like Zoom was not intended for multi-camera video creation, it's very simple to catch a video creation framework result and use it with Zoom. The most straightforward method for utilizing video creation programming and bring it into video conferencing programming is through a HDMI to the USB catch card. A HDMI video catch card can bring that video into programming like Zoom by means of the USB webcam and sound information sources. You can likewise utilize an outer virtual webcam yield with numerous frameworks as well.

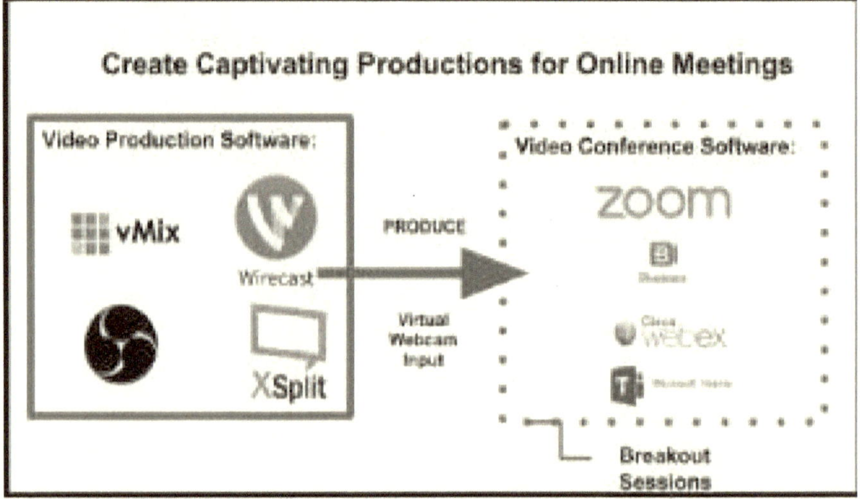

Innovation in the video creation industry has additionally made live streaming and crowd commitment simpler and more intelligent. An organization called vMix has fostered a device called vMix social which coordinates with Facebook, YouTube, Twitch, Twitter, and IRC to oversee remarks that are directed and shown on-screen. The product gives a dashboard to organized online media remarks. It chooses the messages that are consequently overlaid on top of the broadcast.

“Information sources” is another strong element that makes occasions more intuitive. This element permits telecasters to incorporate information sources straightforwardly into on-screen titles. Data sources can incorporate Google Sheets, Excel, RSS, XML, Text, and then some. For instance, your live creation is in progress and there’s a title that is naturally refreshed with opportune data by means of a Google Sheet. The gathering administrator just requirements to enter data straightforwardly into a Google Sheet on their PC or cell phone to have direct admittance to the data being shown on the live transfer or within the video conference.

Here is another model: A non-benefit has a live raising support occasion and acknowledges gifts by means of YouTube Super Chat. The super visits (live donations)
are signed in a Google Sheet which naturally shows the most recent allies of the venture continuously on the live stream.

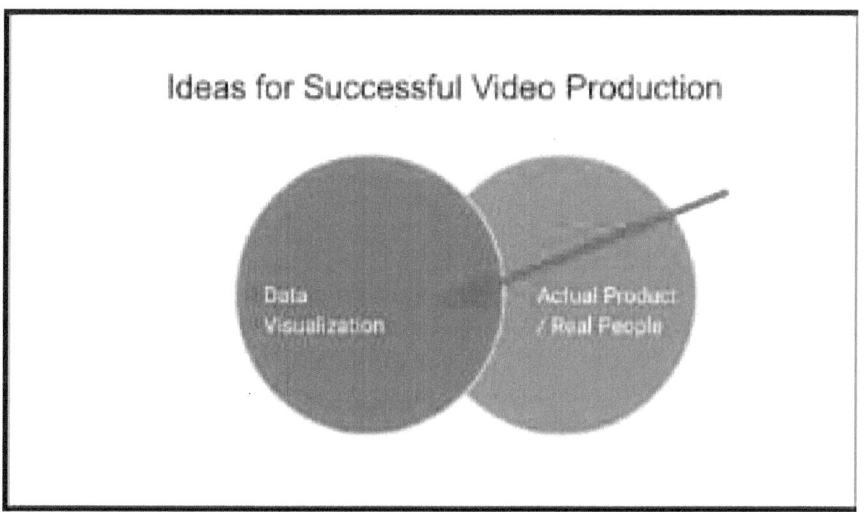

Data visualization and collaboration tools also help educational events find a happy medium between education and entertainment. While charts, graphs, and PowerPoint presentations do a decent job, broadcasters can capture much more audience attention with a mix of data and real-life representations of the data. If you have an app, show the app in detail and share the latest feature. If you sell a product, zoom into the product, and share its look and feel. If you can make your presentation entertaining, you will increase viewer retention.

Consider ways of finding some kind of harmony among data and entertainment.

One especially creative new video creation standard is known as the NewTek NDI. This innovation makes sending and getting excellent video sources over a neighborhood unquestionably simple. Programming like Wirecast, OBS, vMix, Livestream Studio, and a lot more all help this norm. The product permits video creation organizations to get things done to interface standard PCs to make bigger more adaptable frameworks. Alongside IP video creation, IP network for gadgets like PTZ cameras permits more modest groups of makers to help out huge occasions. For instance, PTZOptics cameras support the NewTek NDI and have direct PTZ camera

control mixes with programming like vMix, Wirecast, OBS, Livestream Studio, and NewTek Tricksters. This empowers occasion chiefs to utilize a solitary ethernet link to drive up a camera (by means of PoE), get HD video, and control a PTZ camera.

Note: To look further into the NewTek NDI or PTZOptics cameras consider taking my free courses accessible on Udemy at
- https://www.udemy.com/course/newtek-ndi/

On the substance conveyance organization (CDN) side, developments are beginning to change what's feasible for occasion administrators. Numerous CDNs suppliers presently permit telecasters to adapt their live streams by overlaying moment advertisements on top of the live video transfers. For instance, assuming that your beloved soccer player makes an astonishing objective, telecasters can overlay a connection for where to purchase the player's shirt straightforwardly on top of the video player. Jerk exploits the idea with a component called "Jerk Extensions," a library of instruments that telecasters can use to overlay intuitive components on top of their video players.

Twitch augmentations offer intelligent buttons that show extra data about the videogame as of now being played. For video games that support this integration, viewers can interact with live elements of the game, such as the player's inventory. PTZOptics has an in the background camera control augmentation that gives the crowd control of a PTZ camera. High-profile craftsmen and performers utilize this component to set cameras up behind the stage and charge live watchers for the ability of controlling the crowd's view.

StreamGeeks lives to stay aware of the relative multitude of most recent advancements for live real time, video conferencing, and content conveyance. Since innovation is continually transforming, I suggest joining the StreamGeeks Facebook Group and following our group on friendly media.

Chapter 17: Culture Pushes Us Forward

At a significant level, it's intriguing to check out web-based correspondence according to a social point of view. Human civilization has developed to help huge flooding populaces. Thus, business and economies have thrived, however traffic and over-populace in significant urban areas have turned into an undeniable result of worldwide development. For inventive people and organizations who need to build usefulness at work yet in addition the personal satisfaction through diminished travel, online correspondences have turned into an apparatus essential for growth.

How much worldwide travel the world backings is bewildering. Simply investigate a flight radar site to see plane courses on top of plane courses, flashing all through the world 24 hours per day, 365 days every year. The Covid pandemic has put an impermanent hang on worldwide travel and allowed the world an uncommon opportunity to acquire viewpoint. The strict thunder of the day by day rushing about of current life was decreased to a mumble which permitted us to hear the earth better. Researchers have noted up to a 30 percent decline in worldwide commotion utilizing progressed seismometer machines. Is there something we can gain from the silence?

Ray Oldenburg is a social researcher who can assist us with understanding the significance of public get-together spaces. Oldenburg's work characterizes a significant idea he calls the "Third Place," a social space isolated from home and the work environment. Third places are houses of worship, bistros, recreational areas, and cafés. The Third-Place thought assists us with bettering comprehend the significance of social conditions and their effect on our way of life. Oldenburg's book, *The Great Good Place*, contends that these third places can possibly advance a common society, a majority rules system, and urban commitment. But what happens to a society when our third places are taken away?

Shelter in position orders has constrained a virtual third spot blast through unadulterated need. Need is the mother of development, and through an immense reception of innovation and web access, web-based media, video gaming, and online interchanges have turned into the third spot. One illustration of this was the world's biggest live show with north of 12 million simultaneous watchers that occurred in April 2020 within a computer game.

Fortnite, which is one of the world's most famous computer games, held a virtual show with over 10

million watchers in 2019. There's no live show arena on the planet that could hold even one-10th of the crowd individuals these shows are hosting.

The transition to esports has likewise turned into a worldwide peculiarity for something other than kids playing computer games. With games dropped all over the planet, bicycle races have proceeded with network-associated practice bicycles. Significant association sports are facilitating broadly broadcast computer game forms of booked matches. Zoom video conferencing was utilized during the NFL draft.

Without an uncertainty, zoom video conferencing turned into the online media foundation of the pandemic. North of 20 million individuals every day have downloaded the Zoom application, surprising Google, Microsoft, and Facebook which offer comparable arrangements yet aren't seeing a similar development. At the point when the world requested a space to supplant their in-person associations, Zoom turned into the arrangement that spread like wildfire.

As of April 2020, Facebook had declared a large number of new elements to more readily oblige the new virtual third spot interest. Facebook said it would update its current gathering informing administration to incorporate limitless free video calling for gatherings of up to 50 individuals. Facebook additionally updated its live streaming arrangement which interfaces millions consistently straightforwardly through the online media stage. New highlights for video correspondence and live single direction broadcasting will keep on expanding on the web correspondence in new and creative ways.

So here we've arrived at the end together. Regardless of whether you might want to turn out to be more useful working, invest more energy doing the things you love, or you have an enthusiasm to decrease your carbon impression, online correspondences can assist you with accomplishing these objectives. While the world was going toward this path gradually, the speed at which online correspondences are being embraced will assist us with accomplishing numerous extraordinary things in a short measure of time. Here's to innovation and human ingenuity! I hope that learning how to maximize the use of the various communications tools discussed in this book has helped you to establish good habits and made you a more productive and passionate member of our increasingly connected global community.

Sincerely,

www.ingramcontent.com/pod-product-compliance
Lightning Source LLC
LaVergne TN
LVHW090938150826
845672LV00006B/1555

* 9 7 9 8 4 1 8 5 2 6 2 7 4 *